The F...

In this compelling and provocative book, Walter Lippmann, one of America's leading political thinkers, urgently warns Western man that his liberty is dangerously threatened. In bold, highly readable fashion, he re-examines traditional democratic ideals—freedom of speech, free public education, the enjoyment of private property, and other issues of vital concern to freedom-loving peoples all over the world.

Mr. Lippmann believes that democratic procedures can be safeguarded only by a strong central government, unafraid of the power of mass opinion. Men will continue to be free, he says, only if they elect officials who cannot be bribed, appeased or intimidated by private groups, but who will govern according to the public philosophy, or those principles of unselfish behavior which formed the basis of the U. S. Constitution.

Here is an imaginative, philosophically-grounded discussion which urges every democratic citizen to place the good of his fellow man above personal interest in order to preserve democracy at large, and his own individual liberty.

". . . written with great clarity and deep feeling."
—*Newsweek*

THIS IS A REPRINT OF THE HARDCOVER EDITION ORIGINALLY PUBLISHED BY LITTLE, BROWN AND COMPANY IN ASSOCIATION WITH THE ATLANTIC MONTHLY PRESS.

MENTOR Books of Interest

Democracy in America (abridged) *by Alexis de Tocqueville.* The classic critique of freedom and democracy in 19th century America by a brilliant French political scientist. Specially edited and abridged for the modern reader by Richard D. Heffner. (#MT362—75¢)

The True Believer *by Eric Hoffer.* A provocative analysis of the nature of mass movements and the fanatics who give them power. (#MD228—50¢)

America in Perspective (abridged) *edited by Henry Steele Commager.* Commentary on our national characteristics by twenty-one acute and perceptive foreigners from Tocqueville to Matthew Arnold and Denis W. Brogan. (#MT424—75¢)

American Diplomacy: 1900-1950 *by George F. Kennan.* A trenchant appraisal of U.S. foreign relations by a distinguished diplomat. (#MP360—60¢).

Essays in THE PUBLIC
PHILOSOPHY

by Walter Lippmann

A MENTOR BOOK
Published by THE NEW AMERICAN LIBRARY

*Published as a MENTOR BOOK
By Arrangement with Little, Brown and Company
By Whom the Book Is Published in Association with
The Atlantic Monthly Press*

FIRST PRINTING, MAY, 1956
SECOND PRINTING, APRIL, 1958
THIRD PRINTING, JUNE, 1959
FOURTH PRINTING, JUNE, 1960
FIFTH PRINTING, APRIL, 1961
SIXTH PRINTING, MARCH, 1962

The Public Philosophy is published in England
by Hamish Hamilton, Ltd.

MENTOR TRADEMARK REG. U.S. PAT. OFF. AND FOREIGN COUNTRIES
REGISTERED TRADEMARK—MARCA REGISTRADA
HECHO EN CHICAGO, U.S.A.

*MENTOR BOOKS are published by
The New American Library of World Literature, Inc.
501 Madison Avenue, New York 22, New York*

PRINTED IN THE UNITED STATES OF AMERICA

TO HELEN

They are ill discoverers
that think there is no land,
when they see nothing but sea.

BACON. *Advancement of
Learning,* II: VII, 5

Acknowledgments

ONCE again I am deeply indebted to Edward Weeks, the editor of the *Atlantic Monthly,* for his editorial criticism and for his help in the editing and revision of the text. I can only acknowledge gratefully this debt which I could not repay.

I wish to thank Dean McGeorge Bundy of Harvard University for his very helpful criticism of the text; Mr. Stanley Salmen of Little, Brown for his reassurance and advice; Mr. Curtis W. Cate of the Atlantic Monthly Press for his constructive suggestions, and Dr. Mortimer Adler, Director of the Institute for Philosophical Research, who was consulted when the manuscript was finished, and who offered very prompt assistance with the footnotes and with certain of the logical problems.

W. L.

Washington, D.C.
1954

Contents

Book One: *The Decline of the West*

Book Two: *The Public Philosophy*

BOOK ONE

The Decline of the West

———◆———

CHAPTER ONE

The Obscure Revolution

1. *My Reason for Writing This Book*

DURING the fateful summer of 1938 I began writing a book in an effort to come to terms in my own mind and heart with the mounting disorder in our Western society. I was living in Paris at the time, and I had learned that the decision had been taken which was soon to lead Mr. Chamberlain and Monsieur Daladier to Munich. Little hope remained that another world war could be averted except by abject surrender, and yet there was no sure prospect that France and Great Britain would be able to withstand the onslaught that was coming. They were unprepared, their people were divided and demoralized. The Americans were far away, were determined to be neutral, and were unarmed. I was filled with foreboding that the nations of the Atlantic Community would not prove equal to the challenge, and that, if they failed, we should lose our great traditions of civility,[1] the liberties Western man had won for himself after centuries of struggle and which were now threatened by the rising tide of barbarity.

I began writing, impelled by the need to make more intelligible to myself the alarming failure of the Western liberal democracies to cope with the realities of this century. I had done a draft of the book when the fall of France made it evident that we, too, must soon be engaged

[1] Sir Ernest Barker, *Traditions of Civility* (1948). The phrase is from Coventry Patmore.

11

and, moreover, engaged alone if the Battle of Britain was lost.

But at this time the American people were as unprepared in their minds as in their military establishment. Could the democracies be rallied, could they be collected and nerved for the ordeal so that they would be equal to this mortal challenge? They had the superior assets. They had the numbers, the resources, the influence. But did they have the insight, the discipline to persevere, and the resolution to go through with it? Though they had the means, did they also have the will, and did they still know how? A second world war was making up out of the ruins and the failures of the first, and there was nothing to show that the Western democratic governments were in control of their affairs and capable of making the necessary decisions. They were reacting to events and they were not governing them. Could they avoid defeat and conquest without an exhaustion which would rend the fabric of Western society, without enormities of suffering which would alienate the masses of the people, and without resorting to measures of violence which might become inexpiable? They were so very late, and they were becoming engaged in they knew not what. They had refused to take in what they saw, they had refused to believe what they heard, they had wished and they had waited, hoping against hope.

It did not come easily to one who, like myself, had known the soft air of the world before the wars to recognize and acknowledge the sickness of the Western liberal democracies. Yet as we were being drawn unready and unarmed into the second of the great wars, there was no denying, it seemed to me, that there is a deep disorder in our society which comes not from the machinations of our enemies and from the adversities of the human condition but from within ourselves. I was one of a large company who felt that way. Never doubting that the utmost resistance was imperative and that defeat would be irreparable and intolerable, they were a company who knew in their hearts that by total war our world could not be made safe for democracy nor for the four freedoms. We were, I had come to see, not wounded but sick, and because we were failing to bring order and peace to the world, we were beset by those who believed they have been chosen to succeed us.

2. *1917: The Revolutionary Year*

IN DECEMBER 1941 I put the manuscript away, knowing that so much was going to happen to the world and to me that if ever I went back to the book, it would be to start all over again. When I did come back to it after the war, the foreboding which had inspired it was in a terrible measure realized. Something had gone very wrong in the liberal democracies. They had, to be sure, defeated their enemies. They had avoided defeat and subjection. But they were unable to make peace and to restore order. For the second time in a generation they had failed to prevent a ruinous war, they had been unwilling to prepare themselves to wage the war, and when at long last and at exorbitant cost they had managed to defeat their enemies, they had been unable to make peace out of their victories. They were entangled in a vicious circle of wars that led to ever bigger and wider wars. Could it be denied that they were sick with some kind of incapacity to cope with reality, to govern their affairs, to defend their vital interests and, it might be, to insure their survival as free and democratic states?

There was no mistaking the decline of the West. Thirty years after Wilson had proclaimed a world at peace under democratic governments, the North Atlantic democracies were preoccupied with the defense of western Europe and the fringes of the Eurasian continent. In less than half a century it had come to that. In 1900 men everywhere on earth had acknowledged, even when they resented, the primacy of the Western nations. They were the recognized leaders in the progress of mankind, and it was taken as axiomatic that the question was when, and not whether, the less advanced people would have learned how to use the Western technology, to hold free elections, to respect the Bill of Rights and to live by its political philosophy. Until 1917 the model for a new government anywhere in the world, even in Russia, was liberal democracy in the British, the French, or the American style.

But by the end of 1920 things had taken a sharp turn. Lord Bryce was then finishing his *Modern Democracies,* and though he still wrote in the prewar manner that democracy was spreading and that the number of democracies in the world had doubled within fifteen years, he had seen the warning signs and he was troubled. It might not be "really helpful to the younger generation," he wrote in the preface, but he could not "repress the pessimism of experience." He had to say that "although democracy has spread, and although no country that has tried it shows any signs of forsaking it, we are not yet entitled to hold with the men of 1789 that it is the natural and, therefore, in the long run, the inevitable form of government. Much has happened since the rising sun of liberty dazzled the eyes of the States-General at Versailles. Popular government has not yet been proved to guarantee, always and everywhere, good government. If it be improbable, yet it is not unthinkable that, as in many countries impatience with tangible evils substituted democracy for monarchy or oligarchy, a like impatience might someday reverse the process." [2]

Three years later Mussolini marched on Rome, and Italy became the first of the bigger democracies "to reverse the process." In retrospect we can now see that what Lord Bryce, writing at the end of the First World War, thought was the pessimism of experience was in fact the intuition of a sensitive and knowing observer. He had felt in his bones, being too close to the event to perceive it, that a fundamental change in the prospects of democracy was in the making.

There had occurred, I now believe, an unrecognized revolution within the democratic states. By the third year of the First World War the cumulative losses had become so exorbitant that the institutional order of all the belligerents gave way under the stress and strain. The war had become, in Ferrero's telling phrase, hyperbolic, and the prewar governments were incapable of imposing such unlimited drafts upon the endurance and the loyalties of the people. In the defeated countries the price of this was revolution against the established order. The Romanoff, the Hohenzollern, the Hapsburg and the Ottoman Empires collapsed. In the victorious countries institutions were not overthrown, rulers were not exiled, imprisoned or executed. But the constitutional order was altered subtly and yet radically, within itself.

[2] James Bryce, *Modern Democracies* (1921), Vol. I, p. 42.

3. *Internal Revolution in the Democracies*

A VIGOROUS critic of democracy, Sir Henry Maine, writing in 1884 just as England was about to adopt general manhood suffrage, observed that "there could be no grosser mistake" than the impression that "Democracy differs from Monarchy in essence." For "the tests of success in the performance of the necessary and natural duties of a government are precisely the same in both cases." [3] These natural and necessary duties have to do with the defense and advancement abroad of the vital interests of the state and with its order, security, and solvency at home. Invariably these duties call for hard decisions. They are hard because the governors of the state must tax, conscript, command, prohibit; they must assert a public interest against private inclination and against what is easy and popular. If they are to do their duty, they must often swim against the tides of private feeling.

The hardness of governing was little realized in the early 1900's. For more than half a century, while democracy was making its historic advance, there had been a remarkable interlude during which the governments rarely had to make hard decisions. Since Waterloo there had been no world war, and after the American Civil War only a few short and localized wars. It was a time of expansion, development, liberation; there were new continents to be colonized and there was a new industrial system to be developed. It seemed as though mankind had outlived the tempests of history. The governments—which were increasingly democratic, liberal and humane—were spared the necessity of dealing with the hard issues of war and peace, of security and solvency, of constitutional order and revolution. They could be concerned with improvements, with the more and more and the better and better. Life was secure, liberty was assured, and the way was open to the pursuit of private happiness.

In this long peace, the liberals became habituated to the notion that in a free and progressive society it is a good thing that the government should be weak. For several generations the West had flourished under governments

---

[3] Sir Henry Maine, *Popular Government* (1886), pp. 60-61.

that did not have to prove their strength by making the hard decisions. It had been possible to dream, without being rudely awakened, that in the rivalry of the diverse interests all would somehow come out for the best. The government could normally be neutral and for the most part it could avoid making positive judgments of good and bad and of right and wrong. The public interest could be equated with that which was revealed in election returns, in sales reports, balance sheets, circulation figures, and statistics of expansion. As long as peace could be taken for granted, the public good could be thought of as being immanent in the aggregate of private transactions. There was no need for a governing power which transcended the particular interests and kept them in order by ruling over them.

All this was only, as we now know, a daydream during a brief spell of exceptionally fine weather. The dream ended with the outbreak of the First World War. Then we knew that the Age of Progress had not reformed the human condition of diversity and conflict; it had not mitigated the violence of the struggle for survival and domination.

In fact, the violence was intensified and extended as never before. The expansion and development during the peaceful decades had wrought, as Graham Wallas pointed out on the eve of the war, "a general change of social scale," [4] and that change of scale had revolutionary consequences. The forty years which separated the Franco-Prussian War from the First World War were, says John U. Nef, "in terms of material welfare . . . the most successful years in history . . . In little more than one generation the world's population grew by almost as much as it had grown during the untold generations which separate Adam, the first man, from Newton, the first man of science of the seventeenth century. According to the enterprising calculations of Colin Clark, the real income per person gainfully employed improved 75 per cent or more from 1870 to 1914, while the hours of work were substantially reduced in the wealthier countries of Western Europe . . . and in North America." [5]

Because of the increase in the population, in the volume of production, and in the destructiveness of weapons, the

---

[4] Graham Wallas, *The Great Society*, Ch. I.
[5] John U. Nef, *War and Human Progress*, Ch. 18.

war which brought to an end the Age of Progress had, says Nef, "none of the limiting features of the warfare which had been characteristic of Newton's age. Europe could now afford enormous armies, could replenish and supply them again while the fighting proceeded. More money was needed to kill than ever before, but the money required turned out to be small in comparison with the money that could be raised (with the help of refined advances in the use and manipulation of credit), and in relation to the quantity of munitions which money and credit could buy." All this meant that when war broke out again, the advanced nations had become, as Nickerson says, "capable of sacrifices so irrationally great that the bleeding victor would faint upon the corpse of his victim."[6]

The strain of the war worked up a menacing popular pressure upon the weak governments. We can, I think, point to 1917 as the year when the pressure became so strong that the institutional framework of the established governments broke under it.

The strain became unbearable. 1917 was the year of the two Russian revolutions. It was the year of the American involvement which brought with it the declaration of the Wilsonian principles. For Italy it was the year of Caporetto. For Austria-Hungary it was the beginning of the end under the successor of Francis Joseph. For Germany it was the year of the July crisis and of the need of the Prussian monarchy to listen to the Reichstag and its demand for a negotiated peace. For France it was the year of the mutinies, and for Britain the year of mortal peril from the submarine. In eastern and central Europe tortured and infuriated masses brought down the historic states and the institutions of the old regime. In western Europe and in North America the breakthrough took the form—if I may use the term—of a deep and pervasive infiltration. Behind the façade, which was little changed, the old structure of executive government with the consent of a representative assembly was dismantled—not everywhere and

[6] "In the military massacres of 1914-1915-1916 the French had lost permanently over 900,000 men, the British about half that number, and the Germans well over 800,000 . . . the Russians had mobilized 12,000,000 men and of them at least four million are presumed to have died, another 2,500,000 had become prisoners or were missing and an additional million were seriously wounded." Hoffman Nickerson, *The Armed Horde* (1940), pp. 292-294.

not in all fields, but where it mattered the most—in the
making of high policy for war and peace.

The existing governments had exhausted their imperium
—their authority to bind and their power to command.
With their traditional means they were no longer able to
carry on the hyperbolic war; yet they were unable to
negotiate peace. They had, therefore, to turn to the people.
They had to ask still greater exertions and sacrifices. They
obtained them by "democratizing" the conduct and the
aims of the war: by pursuing total victory and by promising
total peace.

In substance they ceded the executive power of decision
over the strategical and the political conditions for con-
cluding the war. In effect they lost control of the war.
This revolution appeared to be a cession of power to the
representative assemblies, and when it happened it was
acclaimed as promising the end of the evils of secret diplomacy and the undemocratic conduct of unpopular wars.
In fact, the powers which were ceded by the executive
passed through the assemblies, which could not exercise
them, to the mass of voters who, though unable also to
exercise them, passed them on to the party bosses, the
agents of pressure groups, and the magnates of the new
media of mass communications.

The consequences were disastrous and revolutionary.
The democracies became incapacitated to wage war for
rational ends and to make a peace which would be observed or could be enforced.

4. *The Paralysis of Governments*

PERHAPS, before going any further, I should say that I
am a liberal democrat and have no wish to disenfranchise
my fellow citizens. My hope is that both liberty and democracy can be preserved before the one destroys the
other. Whether this can be done is the question of our
time, what with more than half the world denying and
despairing of it. Of one thing we may be sure. If it is to
be done at all, we must be uninhibited in our examination
of our condition. And since our condition is manifestly
connected with grave errors in war and peace that have
been committed by democratic governments, we must
adopt the habit of thinking as plainly about the sovereign
people as we do about the politicians they elect. It will

not do to think poorly of the politicians and to talk with bated breath about the voters. No more than the kings before them should the people be hedged with divinity. Like all princes and rulers, like all sovereigns, they are ill-served by flattery and adulation. And they are betrayed by the servile hypocrisy which tells them that what is true and what is false, what is right and what is wrong, can be determined by their votes.

If I am right in what I have been saying, there has developed in this century a functional derangement of the relationship between the mass of the people and the government. The people have acquired power which they are incapable of exercising, and the governments they elect have lost powers which they must recover if they are to govern. What then are the true boundaries of the people's power? The answer cannot be simple. But for a rough beginning let us say that the people are able to give and to withhold their consent to being governed—their consent to what the government asks of them, proposes to them, and has done in the conduct of their affairs. They can elect the government. They can remove it. They can approve or disapprove its performance. But they cannot administer the government. They cannot themselves perform. They cannot normally initiate and propose the necessary legislation. A mass cannot govern. The people, as Jefferson said, are not "qualified to exercise themselves the Executive Department; but they are qualified to name the person who shall exercise it . . . They are not qualified to legislate; with us therefore they only choose the legislators."[7]

Where mass opinion dominates the government, there is a morbid derangement of the true functions of power. The derangement brings about the enfeeblement, verging on paralysis, of the capacity to govern. This breakdown in the constitutional order is the cause of the precipitate and catastrophic decline of Western society. It may, if it cannot be arrested and reversed, bring about the fall of the West.

The propensity to this derangement and the vulnerability of our society to it have a long and complex history. Yet the more I have brooded upon the events which I have lived through myself, the more astounding and

[7] *Works* (Ford ed. V, pp. 103-104, 1892-1898) cited in Yves R. Simon, *Philosophy of Democratic Government* (1951), p. 169.

significant does it seem that the decline of the power and influence and self-confidence of the Western democracies has been so steep and so sudden. We have fallen far in a short span of time. However long the underlying erosion had been going on, we were still a great and powerful and flourishing community when the First World War began. What we have seen in not only decay—though much of the old structure was dissolving—but something which can be called an historic catastrophe.

CHAPTER TWO

The Malady of Democratic States

1. *Public Opinion in War and Peace*

WRITING in 1913, just before the outbreak of the war, and having in mind Queen Victoria and King Edward the VII, Sir Harry Johnston thus described how foreign affairs were conducted in the Nineteenth Century:

> In those days, a country's relations with its neighbors or with distant lands were dealt with almost exclusively by the head of the State—Emperor, King, or President —acting with the more-or-less dependent Minister-of-State, who was no representative of the masses, but the employé of the Monarch. Events were prepared and sprung on a submissive, a confident, or a stupid people. The public Press criticized, more often applauded, but had at most to deal with a *fait accompli* and make the best of it. Occasionally, in our own land, a statesman, out of office and discontented, went round the great provincial towns agitating against the trend of British foreign policy—perhaps wisely, perhaps unfairly, we do not yet know—and scored a slight success. But once in office, his Cabinet fell in by degrees with the views of the Sovereign and the permanent officials (after the fifties of the last century these public servants were a factor of ever-growing importance); and, as before, the foreign policy of the Empire was shaped by a small camarilla consisting of the Sovereign, two Cabinet Ministers, the permanent Under-Secretary of State for Foreign Affairs, and perhaps one representative of *la plus haute finance*.[1]

Without taking it too literally, this is a fair description of how foreign affairs were conducted before the First World War. There were exceptions. The Aberdeen gov-

[1] Sir Harry Johnston, "Common Sense in Foreign Policy," pp. 1-2, cited in Howard Lee McBain & Lindsay Rogers, *The New Constitutions of Europe* (1922), p. 139.

ernment, for example, was overthrown in 1855 because of its inefficient conduct of the Crimean War. But generally speaking, the elected parliaments were little consulted in the deliberations which led up to war, or on the high strategy of the war, on the terms of the armistice, on the conditions of peace. Even their right to be informed was severely limited, and the principle of the system was, one might say, that war and peace were the business of the executive department. The power of decision was not in, was not even shared with, the House of Commons, the Chamber of Deputies, the Reichstag.

The United States was, of course, a special case. The Congress has always had constitutional rights to advise and to be consulted in the declaration of war and in the ratification of treaties. But at the time I am talking about, that is to say before the First World War broke out, it was American policy to abstain from the role of a great power, and to limit its sphere of vital interests to the Western Hemisphere and the North Pacific Ocean. Only in 1917 did the American constitutional system for dealing with foreign affairs become involved with the conduct of world affairs.

For the reasons which I outlined in the first chapter this system of executive responsibility broke down during the war, and from 1917 on the conduct of the war and then the conditions of the armistice and the peace were subjected to the dominating impact of mass opinions.

Saying this does not mean that the great mass of the people have had strong opinions about the whole range of complex issues which were before the military staffs and the foreign offices. The action of mass opinion has not been, and in the nature of things could not be, continuous through the successive phases in which affairs develop. Action has been discontinuous. Usually it has been a massive negative imposed at critical junctures when a new general course of policy needed to be set. There have, of course, been periods of apathy and of indifference. But democratic politicians have preferred to shun foresight about troublesome changes to come, knowing that the massive veto was latent, and that it would be expensive to them and to their party if they provoked it.

In the winter of 1918-1919, for example, Lloyd George, Clemenceau, Wilson and Orlando were at a critical juncture of modern history. The Germans were defeated, their government was overthrown, their troops disarmed and disbanded. The Allies were called upon to decide whether they would dictate a punitive peace or would negotiate a peace of reconciliation.

In the Thirties the British and the French governments had to decide whether to rearm and to take concerted measures to contain Hitler and Mussolini or whether to remain unarmed and to appease them. The United States had to decide whether to arm in order to contain the Japanese or to negotiate with them at the expense of China.

During the Second World War the British and the American governments had again to make the choice between total victory with unconditional surrender and negotiated settlements whose end was reconciliation.

These were momentous issues, like choosing at the fork of the road a way from which there is no turning back: whether to arm or not to arm—whether, as a conflict blows up, to intervene or to withdraw—whether in war to fight for the unconditional surrender of the adversary or for his reconciliation. The issues are so momentous that public feeling quickly becomes incandescent to them. But they can be answered with the only words that a great mass *qua* mass can speak—with a Yes or a No.

Experience since 1917 indicates that in matters of war and peace the popular answer in the democracies is likely to be No. For everything connected with war has become dangerous, painful, disagreeable and exhausting to very nearly everyone. The rule to which there are few exceptions—the acceptance of the Marshall Plan is one of them —is that at the critical junctures, when the stakes are high, the prevailing mass opinion will impose what amounts to a veto upon changing the course on which the government is at the time proceeding. Prepare for war in time of peace? No. It is bad to raise taxes, to unbalance the budget, to take men away from their schools or their jobs, to provoke the enemy. Intervene in a developing conflict? No. Avoid the risk of war. Withdraw from the area of the conflict? No. The adversary must not be appeased. Reduce your claims on the area? No. Righteousness cannot be compromised. Negotiate a compromise peace as soon as the opportunity presents itself? No. The aggressor must be punished. Remain armed to enforce the dictated settlement? No. The war is over.

The unhappy truth is that the prevailing public opinion

has been destructively wrong at the critical junctures. The people have imposed a veto upon the judgments of informed and responsible officials. They have compelled the governments, which usually knew what would have been wiser, or was necessary, or was more expedient, to be too late with too little, or too long with too much, too pacifist in peace and too bellicose in war, too neutralist or appeasing in negotiation or too intransigent. Mass opinion has acquired mounting power in this century. It has shown itself to be a dangerous master of decisions when the stakes are life and death.

2. *The Compulsion to Make Mistakes*

THE ERRORS of public opinion in these matters have a common characteristic. The movement of opinion is slower than the movement of events. Because of that, the cycle of subjective sentiments on war and peace is usually out of gear with the cycle of objective developments. Just because they are mass opinions there is an inertia in them. It takes much longer to change many minds than to change a few. It takes time to inform and to persuade and to arouse large scattered varied multitudes of persons. So before the multitude have caught up with the old events there are likely to be new ones coming up over the horizon with which the government should be preparing to deal. But the majority will be more aware of what they have just caught up with near at hand than with what is still distant and in the future. For these reasons the propensity to say No to a change of course sets up a compulsion to make mistakes. The opinion deals with a situation which no longer exists.

When the world wars came, the people of the liberal democracies could not be aroused to the exertions and the sacrifices of the struggle until they had been frightened by the opening disasters, had been incited to passionate hatred, and had become intoxicated with unlimited hope. To overcome this inertia the enemy had to be portrayed as evil incarnate, as absolute and congenital wickedness. The people wanted to be told that when this particular enemy had been forced to unconditional surrender, they would re-enter the golden age. This unique war would end all wars. This last war would make the world safe for democracy. This crusade would make the whole world a democracy.

As a result of this impassioned nonsense public opinion became so envenomed that the people would not countenance a workable peace; they were against any public man who showed "any tenderness for the Hun," or was inclined to listen to the "Hun food snivel." [2]

3. *The Pattern of the Mistakes*

IN ORDER to see in its true perspective what happened, we must remember that at the end of the First World War the only victorious powers were the liberal democracies of the West. Lenin, who had been a refugee in Switzerland until 1917, was still at the very beginning of his struggle to become the master of the empire of the Romanoffs. Mussolini was an obscure journalist, and nobody had dreamed of Hitler. The men who took part in the Peace Conference were men of the same standards and tradition. They were the heads of duly elected governments in countries where respect for civil liberty was the rule. Europe from the Atlantic to the Pripet Marshes lay within the military orbit of their forces. All the undemocratic empires, enemy and ally, had been destroyed by defeat and revolution. In 1918—unlike 1945—there had been no Yalta, there was no alien foreign minister at the peace conference who held a veto on the settlement.

Yet as soon as the terms of the settlement were known, it was evident that peace had not been made with Germany. It was not for want of power but for want of statesmanship that the liberal democracies failed. They failed to restore order in that great part of the world which—outside of revolutionary Russia—was still within the orbit of their influence, still amenable to their leadership, still subject to their decisions, still working within the same economy, still living in the same international community, still thinking in the same universe of discourse. In this failure to make peace there was generated the cycle of wars in which the West has suffered so sudden and so spectacular a decline.

Public opinion, having vetoed reconciliation, had made the settlement unworkable. And so when a new genera-

[2] Cf. Harold Nicholson, *Peacemaking,* Chap. III.

tion of Germans grew up, they rebelled. But by that time the Western democracies, so recently too warlike to make peace with the unarmed German Republic, had become too pacifist to take the risks which could have prevented the war Hitler was announcing he would wage against Europe. Having refused the risk of trying to prevent war, they would not now prepare for the war. The European democracies chose to rely on the double negative of unarmed appeasement, and the American democracy chose to rely on unarmed isolation.

When the unprevented war came, the fatal cycle was repeated. Western Europe was defeated and occupied before the British people began seriously to wage the war. And after the catastrophe in Western Europe eighteen agonizing months of indecision elapsed before the surprise and shock of Pearl Harbor did for the American people what no amount of argument and evidence and reason had been able to do.

Once again it seemed impossible to wage the war energetically except by inciting the people to paroxysms of hatred and to utopian dreams. So they were told that the Four Freedoms would be established everywhere, once the incurably bad Germans and the incurably bad Japanese had been forced to surrender unconditionally. The war could be popular only if the enemy was altogether evil and the Allies very nearly perfect. This mixture of envenomed hatred and furious righteousness made a public opinion which would not tolerate the calculated compromises that durable settlements demand. Once again the people were drugged by the propaganda which had aroused them to fight the war and to endure its miseries. Once again they would not think, once again they would not allow their leaders to think, about an eventual peace with their enemies, or about the differences that must arise among the Allies in this coalition, as in all earlier ones. How well this popular diplomacy worked is attested by the fact that less than five years after the democracies had disarmed their enemies, they were imploring their former enemies, Germany and Japan, to rearm.

The record shows that the people of the democracies, having become sovereign in this century, have made it increasingly difficult for their governments to prepare properly for war or to make peace. Their responsible officials have been like the ministers of an opinionated and willful despot. Between the critical junctures, when public opinion has been inattentive or not vehemently aroused, responsible officials have often been able to circumvent extremist popular opinions and to wheedle their way towards moderation and good sense. In the crises, however, democratic officials—over and above their own human propensity to err—have been compelled to make the big mistakes that public opinion has insisted upon. Even the greatest men have not been able to turn back the massive tides of opinion and of sentiment.

There is no mystery about why there is such a tendency for popular opinion to be wrong in judging war and peace. Strategic and diplomatic decisions call for a kind of knowledge—not to speak of an experience and a seasoned judgment—which cannot be had by glancing at newspapers, listening to snatches of radio comment, watching politicians perform on television, hearing occasional lectures, and reading a few books. It would not be enough to make a man competent to decide whether to amputate a leg, and it is not enough to qualify him to choose war or peace, to arm or not to arm, to intervene or to withdraw, to fight on or to negotiate.

Usually, moreover, when the decision is critical and urgent, the public will not be told the whole truth. What can be told to the great public it will not hear in the complicated and qualified concreteness that is needed for a practical decision. When distant and unfamiliar and complex things are communicated to great masses of people, the truth suffers a considerable and often a radical distortion. The complex is made over into the simple, the hypothetical into the dogmatic, and the relative into an absolute. Even when there is no deliberate distortion by censorship and propaganda, which is unlikely in time of war, the public opinion of masses cannot be counted upon to apprehend regularly and promptly the reality of things. There is an inherent tendency in opinion to feed upon rumors excited by our own wishes and fears.

4. *Democratic Politicians*

AT THE critical moments in this sad history, there have been men, worth listening to, who warned the people against their mistakes. Always, too, there have been men inside the governments who judged correctly, because they were permitted to know in time, the uncensored and unvarnished truth. But the climate of modern democracy does not usually inspire them to speak out. For what Churchill did in the Thirties before Munich was exceptional: the general rule is that a democratic politician had better not be right too soon. Very often the penalty is political death. It is much safer to keep in step with the parade of opinion than to try to keep up with the swifter movement of events.

In government offices which are sensitive to the vehemence and passion of mass sentiment public men have no sure tenure. They are in effect perpetual office seekers, always on trial for their political lives, always required to court their restless constituents. They are deprived of their independence. Democratic politicians rarely feel they can afford the luxury of telling the whole truth to the people.[3] And since not telling it, though prudent, is uncomfortable, they find it easier if they themselves do not have to hear too often too much of the sour truth. The men under them who report and collect the news come to realize in their turn that it is safer to be wrong before it has become fashionable to be right.

With exceptions so rare that they are regarded as miracles and freaks of nature, successful democratic politicians are insecure and intimidated men. They advance politically only as they placate, appease, bribe, seduce, bamboozle, or otherwise manage to manipulate the demanding and threatening elements in their constituencies. The decisive consideration is not whether the proposition is good but whether it is popular—not whether it will work well and prove itself but whether the active talking constituents like it immediately. Politicians rationalize this servitude by saying that in a democracy public men are the servants of the people.

---

[3] "As we look over the list of the early leaders of the republic, Washington, John Adams, Hamilton, and others, we discern that they were all men who insisted upon being themselves and who refused to truckle to the people. With each succeeding generation, the growing demand of the people that its elective officials shall not lead but merely register the popular will has steadily undermined the independence of those who derive their power from popular election. The persistent refusal of the Adamses to sacrifice the integrity of their own intellectual and moral standards and values for the sake of winning public office or popular favor is another of the measuring rods by which we may measure the divergence of American life from its starting point." James Truslow Adams, *The Adams Family* (1930), p. 95.

This devitalization of the governing power is the malady of democratic states. As the malady grows the executives become highly susceptible to encroachment and usurpation by elected assemblies; they are pressed and harassed by the higgling of parties, by the agents of organized interests, and by the spokesmen of sectarians and ideologues. The malady can be fatal. It can be deadly to the very survival of the state as a free society if, when the great and hard issues of war and peace, of security and solvency, of revolution and order are up for decision, the executive and judicial departments, with their civil servants and technicians, have lost their power to decide.

CHAPTER THREE

The Derangement of Powers

1. *The Governors and the Governed*

WHEN I describe the malady of democratic states as a derangement in the relation between the mass of the people and the government, I am, of course, implying that there is a sound relationship and that we should be able to know what it is. We must now examine this assumption. We are looking into the relation between, on the one hand, the governing or executive power, and, on the other hand, the elected assembly and the voters in the constituencies. The best place to begin is in the simple beginnings of our constitutional development—in the medieval English Parliament—before the essential functions and their relations had become complicated by their later development.

No relationship, sound or unsound, could exist until the functions of execution and representation had become differentiated. In primitive societies they are not differentiated. Under the Norman and Angevin rulers the differentiation had not yet occurred. These rulers "judged and legislated as well as administered." [1] But by the thirteenth century the differentiation is already visible, and the essential relation in which we are interested can be recognized. There is a writ issued under Henry III in 1254, summoning Parliament. The sheriff of each county is ordered to "cause to come before the King's Council two good and discreet Knights of the Shire, whom the men of the county shall have chosen for this purpose in the stead of all and of each of them, to consider along with knights of other shires what aid they will grant the King." [2]

Let us note the dualism. There is the government, which means the King and his Council of prelates and peers. Then there are the Knights of the Shires, representing

[1] A. F. Pollard, *The Evolution of Parliament* (1926), p. 240.
[2] *Encyclopedia Britannica* (1952), Vol. 19, p. 164, article "Representation."

the men of the counties. They are to meet, and the King will ask the Knights what aid they will grant to him. This is the basic relationship. The government can act. Because it can act, it decides what action should be taken, and it proposes the measures; it then asks the representatives of those who must supply the money and the men for the means to carry out its decisions. The governed, through their representatives, the two Knights of the Shire from each county, give or withhold their consent.

From the tension and the balance of the two powers—that of the ruler and that of the ruled—there evolved the written and the unwritten contracts of the constitution. The grant of aid by the ruled must be preceded by the ruler's redress of their grievances. The government will be refused the means of governing if it does not listen to the petitions, if it does not inform, if it does not consult, if it cannot win the consent of, those who have been elected as the representatives of the governed.

The executive is the active power in the state, the asking and the proposing power. The representative assembly is the consenting power, the petitioning, the approving and the criticizing, the accepting and the refusing power. The two powers are necessary if there is to be order and freedom. But each must be true to its own nature, each limiting and complementing the other. The government must be able to govern and the citizens must be represented in order that they shall not be oppressed. The health of the system depends upon the relationship of the two powers. If either absorbs or destroys the functions of the other power, the constitution is deranged.

There is here a relationship between governors and governed which is, I would contend, rooted in the nature of things. At the risk of reasoning by analogy, I would suggest that this duality of function within a political society has a certain resemblance to that of the two sexes. In the act of reproduction each sex has an unalterable physiological function. If this function is devitalized or is confused with the function of the other sex, the result is sterility and disorder.

In the final acts of the state the issues are war and peace, security and solvency, order and insurrection. In these final acts the executive power cannot be exercised by the representative assembly. Nor can it be exercised after the suppression of the assembly. For in the derangement of the two primary functions lie the seeds of disaster.

2. *The People and the Voters*

A RECENT historian of the Tudor Revolution, Mr. G. R. Elton, says that "our history is still much written by whigs, the champions of political freedom," and that "while the safeguards against despotism have long been understood and often described,—strong rule, preventing anarchy and preserving order, requires still much exploration." There have been periods, he goes on to say, of which the Tudor Age was one—and our own, we may add, is another—when men were so ready to be governed, being so oppressed by disorder, that they have preferred strong government to free government.

The Western liberal democracies are a declining power in human affairs. I argue that this is due to a derangement of the functions of their governments which disables them in coping with the mounting disorder. I do not say, indeed it is impossible to know surely, whether the malady can be cured or whether it must run its course. But I do say that if it cannot be cured, it will continue to erode the safeguards against despotism, and the failure of the West may be such that freedom will be lost and will not be restored again except by another revolution. But for either contingency, for cure now or for recovery after a catastrophe, our first necessity is to work towards an adequate knowledge of the two functions, their nature, and their derangement.

In order to do so it is necessary at the outset to reduce the ambiguity of the term "the people." For it has two different meanings, which it may be convenient to distinguish typographically. When we speak of popular sovereignty, we must know whether we are talking about The People, as voters, or about *The People,* as a community of the entire living population, with their predecessors and successors.

It is often assumed, but without warrant, that the opinions of The People as voters can be treated as the expression of the interests of *The People* as an historic community. The crucial problem of modern democracy arises from the fact that this assumption is false. The voters cannot be relied upon to represent *The People*. The opinions of voters in elections are not to be accepted unquestioningly as true judgments of the vital interests of the community.

To whom, for example, did the Preamble of the Constitution refer when it said that "We, the People of the United States . . . ordain and establish this Constitution"? On September 17, 1787, about forty members signed the draft on which they had been working since May 25, for one hundred and sixteen days. In Article VII of their text they stipulated that if and when conventions in nine states had ratified it, then for those nine states The People of the United States would have ordained and established the Constitution. In this context a majority of the delegates elected to nine state conventions were deemed to be entitled to act as The People of the United States.

The inhabitants of the United States who were qualified to vote for these delegates were not a large number. They included no slaves, no women and, except in New York, only such adult males as could pass property and other highly restrictive tests. We do not have accurate figures. But according to the census of 1790 the population was 3,929,782. Of these, 3,200,000 were free persons and the adult males among them who were entitled to vote are estimated to have been less than 500,000. Using the Massachusetts figures as a statistical sample, it may be assumed that less than 160,000 actually voted for delegates to all the ratifying conventions; and of those voting, perhaps 100,000 favored the adoption of the Constitution.[3]

The exact figures do not matter. The point is that the voters were not—and we may add that they have never been and can never be—more than a fraction of the total population. They were less than 5 per cent when the Constitution was ordained. They were not yet 40 per cent in 1952 when, except under the special conditions in the South, we had universal adult suffrage. Manifestly,

[3] These figures are from a memorandum prepared for me by my friend, Prof. Allan Nevins. In his covering letter, January 24, 1952, he says:

"Anyone who writes about election figures in our early national history treads upon very unsafe ground. Trustworthy data—the statistics and the general information—are too scanty for any explicit statement of detailed conclusions for the country as a whole. As you will see, I have found figures for various states and localities, but we have no warrant for generalizing them to apply to the country in its entirety. *What we can say with absolute certainty, I think, is that in these early elections the vote was under 5 per cent of the whole population.*"

the voters can never be equal to the whole population, even to the whole living adult population.

Because of the discrepancy between The People as voters and *The People* as the corporate nation, the voters have no title to consider themselves the proprietors of the commonwealth and to claim that their interests are identical with the public interest. A prevailing plurality of the voters are not *The People*. The claim that they are is a bogus title invoked to justify the usurpation of the executive power by representative assemblies and the intimidation of public men by demagogic politicians. In fact demagoguery can be described as the sleight of hand by which a faction of The People as voters are invested with the authority of *The People*. That is why so many crimes are committed in the people's name.

There are eminent political philosophers who reject this analytical distinction. Those who are strongly nominalist in their cast of mind, which modern men tend to be, look upon the abstract concept of a corporate people as mere words and rather like conjuring up spooks. Thus, according to that resolute nominalist, Jeremy Bentham, "the community is a fictitious *body,* composed of the individual persons who are considered as constituting as it were its *members*. The interest of the community then is, what?—The sum of the interests of the several members who compose it." [4]

There is an apparent toughness and empirical matter-of-factness in this statement. But the hard ice is thin. For Bentham has forgotten that "the several members who compose" the community are never identically the same members from one hour to another. If a community were what he says it is, then in theory it should be possible to make a directory of its members, each with his address. But no such list could ever be compiled. While it was being compiled, new members would be being born and old members would be dying. That is why it makes no sense to describe "The People of the United States" who ordained and established the Constitution as the inhabitants of the United States on that particular June 21, 1788, when the Constitution was established and ordained. Between sunrise and sunset of that historic day the persons composing *The People* had changed. In thirty

[4] Jeremy Bentham, *The Principles of Morals and Legislation,* Ch. I, Sec. IV.

years they had changed greatly; and in a hundred years, entirely.

The people, then, is not only, as Bentham assumed, the aggregate of living persons. The people is also the stream of individuals, the connected generations of changing persons, that Burke was talking about when he invoked the partnership "not only between those who are living" but also with "those who are dead, and those who are to be born." *The People* are a corporation, an entity, that is to say, which lives on while individuals come into it and go out of it.

For this reason Bentham cannot have been right when he said that the interests of the community are no more than the sum of the interests of the several members who happen to compose it at any particular instant of time. He cannot have been right when he said that "the happiness of the individuals, of whom a community is composed, that is their pleasures and their security, is the end and the sole end which the legislator ought to have in view."[5]

For besides the happiness and the security of the individuals of whom a community is at any moment composed, there are also the happiness and the security of the individuals of whom generation after generation it will be composed. If we think of it in terms of individual persons, the corporate body of *The People* is for the most part invisible and inaudible. Indeed as a whole it is nonexistent, in that so many are dead and so many are not yet born. Yet this corporate being, though so insubstantial to our senses, binds, in Burke's words, a man to his country with "ties which though light as air, are as strong as links of iron."[6] That is why young men die in battle for their country's sake and why old men plant trees they will never sit under.

This invisible, inaudible, and so largely nonexistent community gives rational meaning to the necessary objectives of government. If we deny it, identifying the people with the prevailing pluralities who vote in order to serve, as Bentham has it, "their pleasures and their security," where and what is the nation, and whose duty and business is it to defend the public interest? Bentham leaves us with the state as an arena in which factions contend for their immediate advantage in the struggle for

---

[5] *Ibid.*, Ch. III, Sec. I.
[6] Edmund Burke's speech on *Conciliation with America* (1775).

survival and domination. Without the invisible and transcendent community to bind them, why should they care for posterity? And why should posterity care about them, and about their treaties and their contracts, their commitments and their promises? Yet without these engagements to the future, they could not live and work; without these engagements the fabric of society is unraveled and shredded.

3. *The Recently Enfranchised Voters*

THE DOCTRINE of popular sovereignty is ancient and venerable. But until about the second half of the Nineteenth Century, it did not imply the enfranchisement of the people. When, for example, Charlemagne was crowned in 800 A.D., the Pope professed to be declaring the will of the people. This has been called the principle of "virtual representation."[7] Those who do not vote because they lack the franchise, or cannot vote because they are infants or even unborn, are presumed to be represented by someone like the Pope, the king, the parliament, speaking in their name.

By the coronation of 800 A.D. the empire was being transferred from the Greeks to the Germans. A reason was needed to explain why a German prince, rather than the Emperor of Byzantium, was to be henceforth the lawful successor of the Roman Caesars. The office of emperor was not hereditary, and in any event Charlemagne could have made no claim of kinship; the emperor was not appointed by the Pope; he was chosen by the German princes who belonged to the College of Electors. A doctrine was necessary which would justify and could compel everyone to believe that Charlemagne was the legitimate successor of Caesar.

The publicists of the new empire took for a foundation the accepted theory that "the Imperial power, as successor to the Imperium of the Roman Caesars, was founded originally on an act of transference performed by the people in the Lex Regia."[8] They argued that what had happened

---

[7] The great exponent of "virtual representation" was Burke. Cf. his speech (1784) *On the Reform of the Representation of the Commons in Parliament.*

[8] Otto von Gierke, *The Development of Political Theory,* translated by Bernard Freyd (1939; original first published 1880), p. 92.

once at the beginning of the imperial power would have to happen again whenever the throne was vacant. As the imperium "escheats or reverts to the people"; and the people had then to choose a new emperor, they might even "translate" the empire from one nation to another, in this instance from the Greeks to the Germans. Needless to say, "the people," who were presumed to have this power, had neither votes nor any other means of making their will known. It was presumed that they wished to have their power exercised for them. In the coronation of Charlemagne, the Pope did this: he "merely declared and exercised the people's will."

All this seems long ago and far away. But if we reject virtual representation, the question remains: if the Pope or the king, or the parliament of magnates, cannot represent *The People,* how do a plurality of voters truly declare and exercise *The People's* will? It sounds incongruous to modern ears that the Pope should represent the people. But is it so congruous that the people should be represented by a count of the votes of some persons? The conundrum springs from the fact that while *The People* as a corporate body are the true owners of the sovereign power, The People, as an aggregate of voters, have diverse, conflicting self-centered interests and opinions. A plurality of them cannot be counted upon to represent the corporate nation.

The distinction upon which I am dwelling does not, as one might suppose, cease to matter when the voters become enormously many. Cannot a multitude of voters be regarded as the practical equivalent of all the people? They cannot be. To multiply the voters makes it no more probable that a plurality of them will truly represent the public interest. Our experience with mass elections in the twentieth century compels us, I think, to the contrary conclusion: that public opinion becomes less realistic as the mass to whom information must be conveyed, and argument must be addressed, grows larger and more heterogeneous.

All this will seem less odd if we remind ourselves that political democracy, as we know it in this century, is a very recent political phenomenon. The moral presumption in favor of universal suffrage may perhaps be said to have been laid down by the American and the French Revolutions at the end of the eighteenth century. But (until the end of the nineteenth century) the actual advance towards universal suffrage was in fact spasmodic and slow. In 1900, voters in the United Kingdom were only 11 per cent of the population: they were 43 per cent in 1922. The Representation of The People Act in 1918 had very nearly tripled the electorate by simplifying the extremely complex regulations for voting and by extending the suffrage to women thirty years of age and qualified as occupants. In France the voters were 27 per cent of the population in the election of 1881; in 1951 they were 45 per cent. Until the last quarter of the nineteenth century, in most of Western and Northern Europe, the proportion of voters to population was not more than 5 per cent. In 1890 voters in the United States were about 15 per cent of the population. It has been only since the First World War, owing to the enfranchisement of women and, in some measure, of southern Negroes, that the proportion has risen to over 30 per cent.

Large mass electorates are something quite new, much newer than the ideals, the ideas, the institutions and the usages of the liberal state. Political orators often assume that the mass of the people voted their own liberties. But the fact is that they acquired the vote after they had acquired their liberties and, in fact, largely because not being able to vote was felt by free men to be incompatible with their equal dignity.[9] The Bill of Rights (1689) is more than two centuries older than universal suffrage in Great Britain. The enfranchised people did not establish the rule that all powers are under the law, that laws must be made, amended and administered by due process, that a legitimate government must have the consent of the governed.

I dwell upon this point because it throws light upon the fact, so disconcerting an experience in this century, that the enfranchised masses have not, surprisingly enough, been those who have most stanchly defended the institutions of freedom.

[9] James Bryce, *Modern Democracies,* Vol. I, Ch. IV. Cf. also John Stuart Mill, *Considerations on Representative Government.* In *On Liberty, Representative Government, The Subjection of Women* (London, Oxford University Press, 1946), Ch. VIII, pp. 272-294.

CHAPTER FOUR

The Public Interest

1. *What Is the Public Interest?*

WE ARE examining the question of how, and by whom, the interest of an invisible community over a long span of time is represented in the practical work of governing a modern state.

In ordinary circumstances voters cannot be expected to transcend their particular, localized and self-regarding opinions. As well expect men laboring in the valley to see the land as from a mountain top. In their circumstances, which as private persons they cannot readily surmount, the voters are most likely to suppose that whatever seems obviously good to them must be good for the country, and good in the sight of God.

I am far from implying that the voters are not entitled to the representation of their particular opinions and interests. But their opinions and interests should be taken for what they are and for no more. They are not—as such—propositions in the public interest. Beyond their being, if they are genuine, a true report of what various groups of voters are thinking, they have no intrinsic authority. The Gallup polls are reports of what people are thinking. But that a plurality of the people sampled in the poll think one way has no bearing upon whether it is sound public policy. For their opportunities of judging great issues are in the very nature of things limited, and the statistical sum of their opinions is not the final verdict on an issue. It is, rather, the beginning of the argument. In that argument their opinions need to be confronted by the views of the executive, defending and promoting the public interest. In the accommodation reached between the two views lies practical public policy.

Let us ask ourselves, How is the public interest discerned and judged? From what we have been saying we know that we cannot answer the question by attempting to forecast what the invisible community, with all its unborn constituents, will, would, or might say if and when it ever had a chance to vote. There is no point in toying with any notion of an imaginary plebiscite to discover the public interest. We cannot know what we ourselves will be thinking five years hence, much less what infants now in the cradle will be thinking when they go into the polling booth.

Yet their interests, as we observe them today, are within the public interest. Living adults share, we must believe, the same public interest. For them, however, the public interest is mixed with, and is often at odds with, their private and special interests. Put this way, we can say, I suggest, that the public interest may be presumed to be what men would choose if they saw clearly, thought rationally, acted disinterestedly and benevolently.

2. The Equations of Reality

A RATIONAL man acting in the real world may be defined as one who decides where he will strike a balance between what he desires and what can be done. It is only in imaginary worlds that we can do whatever we wish. In the real world there are always equations which have to be adjusted between the possible and the desired. Within limits, a man can make a free choice as to where he will strike the balance. If he makes his living by doing piecework, he can choose to work harder and to spend more. He can also choose to work less and to spend less. But he cannot spend more and work less.

Reality confronts us in practical affairs as a long and intricate series of equations. What we are likely to call "facts of life" are the accounts, the budgets, the orders of battle, the election returns. Sometimes, but not always, the two sides of the equations can be expressed quantitatively in terms of money, as supply and demand, as income and outgo, assets and liabilities, as exports and imports. Valid choices are limited to the question of where, not whether, the opposing terms of the equation are to be brought into equilibrium. For there is always a reckoning.

In public life, for example, the budget may be balanced by reducing expenditures to the revenue from taxes; by raising taxes to meet the expenditures, or by a combination of the two, by borrowing, or by grants in aid from other governments, or by fiat credit, or by a combination of them. In one way or another the budget is in fact always balanced. The true nature of the reckoning would be clearer if, instead of talking about "an unbalanced budget," we spoke of a budget balanced not by taxes but by borrowing, of a budget balanced by inflation, or of a budget balanced by subsidy. A government which cannot raise enough money by taxes, loans, foreign grants, or by getting its fiat money accepted, will be unable to meet its bills and to pay the salaries of its employees. In bankruptcy an involuntary balance is struck for the bankrupt. He is forced to balance his accounts by reducing his expenditures to the level of his income.

Within limits, which public men have to bear in mind, the choices as to where to balance the budget are open. In making these choices, new equations confront them. Granted that it is possible to bring the budget into balance by raising taxes, how far can taxes be raised? Somewhat but not ad infinitum. There are no fixed criteria. But though we are unable to express all the equations quantitatively, this does not relieve us of the necessity of balancing the equations. There will be a reckoning. Practical judgment requires an informed guess: what will the taxpayers accept readily, what will they accept with grumbling but with no worse, what will arouse them to resistance and to evasion? How will the taxpayers react to the different levels of taxes if it is a time of peace, a time of war, a time of cold war, a time of social and economic disturbance, and so on? Although the various propositions cannot be reduced to precise figures, prudent men make estimates as to where the equations balance.

Their decisions as to where to balance the accounts must reflect other judgments—as to what, for example, are the military requirements in relation to foreign affairs; what is the phase of the business cycle in relation to the needs for increased or decreased demand; what is the condition of the international monetary accounts; which are the necessary public works and welfare measures, and which are those that are desirable but not indispensable. Each of these judgments is itself the peak of a pyramid of equations: whether, for example, to enlarge or to reduce the national commitments at this or that point in the world—given the effect of the decision at other points in the world.

We may say, then, that public policy is made in a field of equations. The issues are the choices as to where the balance is to be struck. In the reality of things X will exact an equivalence of Y. Within the limits which the specific nature of the case permits—limits which have to be estimated—a balance has to be reached by adding to or subtracting from the terms of the equation.

Oftener than not, the two sides of the equation differ in that the one is, as compared with the other, the pleasanter, the more agreeable, the more popular. In general the softer and easier side reflects what we desire and the harder reflects what is needed in order to satisfy the desire. Now the momentous equations of war and peace, of solvency, of security and of order, always have a harder or a softer, a pleasanter or a more painful, a popular or an unpopular option. It is easier to obtain votes for appropriations than it is for taxes, to facilitate consumption than to stimulate production, to protect a market than to open it, to inflate than to deflate, to borrow than to save, to demand than to compromise, to be intransigent than to negotiate, to threaten war than to prepare for it.

Faced with these choices between the hard and the soft, the normal propensity of democratic governments is to please the largest number of voters. The pressure of the electorate is normally for the soft side of the equations. That is why governments are unable to cope with reality when elected assemblies and mass opinions become decisive in the state, when there are no statesmen to resist the inclination of the voters and there are only politicians to excite and to exploit them.

There is then a general tendency to be drawn downward, as by the force of gravity, towards insolvency, towards the insecurity of factionalism, towards the erosion of liberty, and towards hyperbolic wars.

CHAPTER FIVE

The Two Functions

1. *The Elected Executive*

OUR INQUIRY has shown, I believe, that we cannot take popular government for granted, as if its principles were settled and beyond discussion. We are compelled to agree with Sir Henry Maine who wrote, some seventy years ago, that "the actual history of popular government since it was introduced, in its modern shape, into the civilized world," does "little to support the assumption that popular government has an indefinitely long future before it. Experience rather tends to show that it is characterized by great fragility, and that since its appearance, all forms of government have become more insecure than they were before."[1]

We have been dwelling upon the devitalization of the executive power as the cause of the fragility that Maine speaks of. It is, I have been saying, the disorder which results from a functional derangement in the relationship between the executive power on the one hand, the representative assemblies and the mass electorates on the other hand.

Democratic states are susceptible to this derangement because congenitally the executive, when dependent on election, is weaker than the elected representatives The normal drainage of power in a democratic state is away from the governing center and down into the constituencies.[2] And the normal tendency of elections is to reduce elected officers to the role of agents or organized pluralities. Mod-

---

[1] Sir Henry Maine, *Popular Government* (1886), p. 20.

[2] Yves R. Simon, *Philosophy of Democratic Government*, p. 136, quotes Jefferson, *Notes on Virginia* (Memorial ed.; Washington, 1903), Vol. II, pp. 162-163 (the writer is surveying what he terms the "capital defects of the constitution"): "All the powers of government, legislative, executive, and judiciary, result to the legislative body. The concentrating these in the same hands is precisely the definition of despotic government. It will be no alleviation that these powers will be exercised by a plurality of hands, and not by a single one. One hundred and seventy-three despots would surely

ern democratic governments are, to be sure, big governments, in their personnel, in the range and variety of their projects, the ubiquitousness of their interventions. But to be big is not necessarily to be strong. They are, in fact, swollen rather than strong, being too weak to resist the pressure of special interests and of the departmental bureaucracies.

As a rule competition in the electoral market works like Gresham's law: the soft money drives the hard money out of circulation. The competitive odds are heavily against the candidate who, like Burke with the electors of Bristol, promises to be true to his own best reason and judgment. The odds are all in favor of the candidate who offers himself as the agent, the delegate, the spokesman, the errand boy, of blocs of voters.

In a modern democratic state, the chief executive office must be elective. But as heredity, prescription, consecration, rank and hierarchy are dissolved by the acids of modernity, the executives become totally dependent on election. They have no status and no tenure which reinforce their consciences, which invest them with power to withstand the tides of popular opinion and to defend the public interest.

They hold their offices for a short time, and to do this they must maneuver and manipulate combinations among the factions and the pressure groups. Their policies must be selected and shaped so as to attract and hold together these combinations. There are moments, the "finest hours," when communities are lifted above their habitual selves in unity and fellowship. But these moments are rare. They are not the stuff of daily life in a democracy, and they are remembered like a miracle in a dream. In the daily routine of democratic politics, elected executives can never for long take their eyes from the mirror of the constituencies. They must not look too much out of the window at the realities beyond.

---

be as oppressive as one. Let those who doubt it turn their eyes on the republic of Venice. As little will it avail us that they are chosen by ourselves. An *elective despotism* was not the government we fought for, but one which should not only be founded on free principles, but in which the powers of government should be so divided and balanced among several bodies of magistracy, as that no one could transcend their legal limits, without being effectually checked and restrained by the others."

2. *The Protection of the Executive*

DURING the nineteenth century good democrats were primarily concerned with insuring representation in the assemblies and with extending the control of the assemblies over the executive power. It is true that the problem of the inadequate executive, overridden and dominated by the assembly, was very much in the minds of the Founding Fathers at the Philadelphia convention, and it has been a continuing concern of the critics and opponents of democracy. But until the twentieth century the problem was not sharply and urgently posed. That there was such a problem was well known. But it was not the immediate problem.[3]

For some generations before 1914, the West enjoyed fine political weather. Moreover, the full force of the coming enfranchisement, emancipation, and secularization of the whole population had not yet worked its consequences. Governments still had authority and power, which were independent of the assemblies and the electorates. They still drew upon the traditional sources of authority—upon prescription, hereditary prerogative, and consecration.

Yet the need to protect the executive and judicial powers from the representative assemblies and from mass opinion has long been understood.[4] Many expedients have been devised to soften, to neutralize, to check and to balance the pressure of parties, factions, lobbies, sects. The expedients have taken, says Bryce, two general forms, the one being to put constitutional restrictions upon the assembly and the other, "by a division of the whole power of the people," to weaken it.[5] This has been done by electing the legislature and the executive separately, or by having the legislative bodies elected by the differing constituencies and at different times.

The constitutional mechanisms have never themselves been sufficient to protect the executive. And much invention and reforming energy have been applied to finding

[3] But cf. Woodrow Wilson, *Congressional Government,* Ch. 5.
[4] Hamilton, Jay, Madison, *The Federalist,* (Modern Library), No. 48, pp. 322-326; No. 49, pp. 330-332; No. 71, pp. 464-466.
[5] James Bryce, *Modern Democracies* (1921), Vol. II, Ch. LXIII.

other ways to insulate the judicial, the executive and the administrative functions from the heavy pressures of "politics" and "politicians." The object has been to separate them from the electoral process. The judiciary must be independent of fear and favor. There must be no connection between the judgment of the courts and the election returns. The civil service, the military services, the foreign service, the scientific and technical services, the quasi-judicial administrative tribunals, the investigating commissions, the public schools and institutions of learning, should be substantially independent of the elections. These reforms were inspired by the dire effects of the spoils system, and they were pushed as practical remedies for obvious evils.

Yet implicit in them there is a principle which, if it can be applied deeply enough, gets at the root of the disorder of modern democracy. It is that though public officials are elected by the voters, or are appointed by men who are elected, they owe their primary allegiance not to the opinions of the voters but to the law, to the criteria of their professions, to the integrity of the arts and sciences in which they work, to their own conscientious and responsible convictions of their duty within the rules and the frame of reference they have sworn to respect.

3. *The Voters and the Executive*

THE IMPLIED principle may be defined in other terms by saying that while the electors choose the ruler, they do not own any shares in him and they have no right to command him. His duty is to the office and not to his electors. Their duty is to fill the office and not to direct the officeholder. I realize that, as I have stated it, the principle runs counter to the popular view that in a democracy public men are the servants (that is, the agents) of the people (that is, of the voters). As the game of politics is played, what I am saying must seem at first like a counsel of perfection.

There are, however, reasons for thinking that it is not an abstract and empty bit of theorizing. One is that until comparatively recent times, it has been the principle on which the election of rulers—lay and spiritual—has usually been carried out.

In the early church, says Acts VI, the twelve apostles

called the multitude of the disciples to them and said, "Look ye out among you seven men of honest report, full of the Holy Ghost and wisdom, whom we may appoint over this business." When these men had been chosen, and had prayed, "the apostles . . . laid their hands upon them." Having been ordained, they were not the servants of the multitude who had elected them, but of God.

This principle applied to the election of Popes. As Suarez says, "The Pope is elected by cardinals, yet he receives his powers from God immediately."[6] The same principle applied to elected kings. After the electors had chosen the king, he was crowned and anointed. Then his duty was to his own vows and not to the electors. The act of election did not bind the ruler to the electors. Both parties to the transaction were bound only to the office; the electors to designate a king worthy of the office, the king to fill the office worthily.

If we look closely at the matter, we find, I believe, this must be the principle of election when the electors are choosing, not someone to represent them to the government, but the governors themselves. Though it is not too well recognized, there is a radical difference between the election of an executive and the election of a representative. For while the executive is in honor bound not to consider himself as the agent of his electors, the representative is expected to be, within the limits of reason and the general public interest, their agent.[7]

This distinction has deep roots in the political experience of Western society, and, though unrecognized in principle, it is implicit in our moral judgments. Everyone who has a case in court is entitled, we believe, to be represented by a lawyer who, within the law and the code of professional practice, is expected to be the partisan and advocate of his client. But this presupposes not only that his opponent will be effectively represented too, but that the case will go to a court where the judge is not an advocate and has no clients. The judge is bound by his judicial vows. The same ethical standards are recognized, though they are applied less rigorously, in the executive branch of the government. No President or head of a department could afford to admit that he was using his office to further the interests of a client or of a pressure group, or

---

[6] Yves R. Simon, *op. cit.*, p. 174.

[7] Hamilton, Jay, Madison, *op. cit.*, No. 10, pp. 55-62.

even his party. His acts must be presented as taken in obedience to his oath of office, which means taken disinterestedly and rationally. He must never in so many words admit that in order to gain votes he sacrificed the public good, that he played "politics." Often enough he does just that. But fealty to the public interest is his virtue. And he must, at the very least, pay it the homage of hypocrisy.

When we move over to the representative assembly, the image is different, and the ethical rule is applied, if at all, loosely and lightly. The representative is in some very considerable degree an agent, and the image of his virtue is rather like that of the lawyer than of the judge. There are, of course, occasions when he is in fact the holder of one of the great offices of state—as when he must speak and vote on a declaration of war and the ratification of a treaty. But in the general run of the mundane business which comes before the assembly, he is entitled, indeed he is in duty bound, to keep close to the interests and sentiments of his constituents, and, within reasonable limits, to do what he can to support them. For it is indispensable to the freedom and the order of a civilized state that the voters should be effectively represented. But representation must not be confused with governing.

4. *The Enfeebled Executive*

IN THE effort to understand the malady of democratic government I have dwelt upon the underlying duality of functions: *governing,* that is, the administration of the laws and the initiative in legislating, and *representing* the living persons who are governed, who must pay, who must work, who must fight and, it may be, die for the acts of the government. I attribute the democratic disaster of the twentieth century to a derangement of these primary functions.

The power of the executive has become enfeebled, often to the verge of impotence, by the pressures of the representative assembly and of mass opinions. This derangement of the governing power has forced the democratic states to commit disastrous and, it could be, fatal mistakes. It has also transformed the assemblies in most, perhaps not in all, democratic states from the defenders of local and personal rights into boss-ridden oligarchies, threatening the security, the solvency, and the liberties of the state.

In the traditions of Western society, civilized government is founded on the assumption that the two powers exercising the two functions will be in balance—that they will check, restrain, compensate, complement, inform and vitalize each one the other.

In this century, the balance of the two powers has been seriously upset. Two great streams of evolution have converged upon the modern democracies to devitalize, to enfeeble, and to eviscerate the executive powers. One is the enormous expansion of public expenditure, chiefly for war and reconstruction; this has augmented the power of the assemblies which vote the appropriations on which the executive depends. The other development which has acted to enfeeble the executive power is the growing incapacity of the large majority of the democratic peoples to believe in intangible realities. This has stripped the government of that imponderable authority which is derived from tradition, immemorial usage, consecration, veneration, prescription, prestige, heredity, hierarchy.

At the beginning of our constitutional development the King, when he had mastered the great barons, was the proprietor of the greatest wealth in the realm. The crown was also the point from which radiated the imponderable powers to bind and to command. As the King needed money and men for his wars, he summoned representatives of the counties and the boroughs, who had the money and the men he needed. But the imponderable powers, together with very considerable power in land and in men, were still in the King's own hands. Gradually, over the centuries, the power of the Parliament over the supplies of the government grew larger. They had to appropriate a larger proportion of a much greater total. At the same time, in the white light of the enlightenment and the secularization of men's minds, the imponderable powers of the crown diminished.

Under the stress and the strain of the great wars of the twentieth century, the executive power has become elaborately dependent upon the assemblies for its enormous expenditures of men and of money. The executive has, at the same time, been deprived of very nearly all of his imponderable power: fearing the action of the representative assembly, he is under great temptation to outwit it or bypass it, as did Franklin D. Roosevelt in the period of the Second World War. It is significant, I think, certainly it is at least suggestive, that while nearly all the Western governments have been in deep trouble since the First World War, the constitutional monarchies of Scandinavia, the Low Countries, and the United Kingdom have shown greater capacity to endure, to preserve order with freedom, than the republics of France, Germany, Spain and Italy. In some measure that may be because in a republic the governing power, being wholly secularized, loses much of its prestige; it is stripped, if one prefers, of all the illusions of intrinsic majesty.

The evaporation of the imponderable powers, a total dependence upon the assemblies and the mass electorates, has upset the balance of powers between the two functions of the state. The executive has lost both its material and its ethereal powers. The assemblies and the mass electorate have acquired the monopoly of effective powers.

This is the internal revolution which has deranged the constitutional system of the liberal democratic states.

CHAPTER SIX

The Totalitarian Counterrevolution

1. *Certain of Its Lessons*

WE CAN learn something about the kind of incapacity which has brought on disaster for the modern democracies by the nature of the counterrevolutions that have undermined and overthrown so many of them. There are various types of counterrevolutions. The most notable are the Soviet Communist, Italian Fascist, German National Socialist, Spanish Falangist, Portuguese Corporatist, the Titoist, and Peronist. . . . Besides these organized counterrevolutionary movements, professing doctrines of an antiliberal and undemocratic character, there is, in large areas of the world, a very strong tendency to nullify the democratic system behind the façade of democratic institutions. The countries where elections are free and genuine, where civil liberty is secure, are still powerful. But they embrace a shrinking minority of mankind.

Now in all these counterrevolutionary movements there are two common characteristics. One is the separation of the governing power from the large electorate. In the totalitarian states this is done by not holding free elections; in the great number of nontotalitarian but also nondemocratic states, it is done by controlling and rigging the elections.

The other common characteristic of the counterrevolutions is that political power, which is taken away from the electorate, the parties and the party bosses, is then passed to an elite corps marked off from the mass of the people by special training and by special vows. The totalitarian revolutions generally liquidate the elite of the old regime, and then recruit their own elite of specially trained and specially dedicated and highly disciplined men. Elsewhere, when the liberal democratic system fails, the new rulers are drawn from the older established elites—from the army officers, from the clergy, the higher bureaucracy and the diplomatic corps, from university professors.

It is significant that in the reaction against the practical failure of the democratic states, we find always that the electoral process is shut down to a minimum or shut off entirely, and that the executive function is taken over—more often than not with popular assent—by men with a special training and a special personal commitment to the business of ruling the state. In the enfeebled democracies the politicians have with rare exceptions been men without sure tenure of office. Many of the most important are novices, improvisers, and amateurs. After a counter-revolution has brought them down, their successors are almost certain to be either the elite of the new revolutionary party, or an elite drawn from predemocratic institutions like the army, the church, and the bureaucracy.

In their different ways—which ideologically may be at opposite ends of the world—the post-democratic rulers are men set apart from the masses of the people. They are not set apart only because they have the power to arrest others and to shoot them. They would not long hold on to that kind of power. They have also an aura of majesty, which causes them to be obeyed. That aura emanates from the popular belief that they have subjected themselves to a code and are under a discipline by which they are dedicated to ends that transcend their personal desires and their own private lives.

2. *A Prognosis*

THE NATURE of the counterrevolution reflects a radical deficiency in the modern liberal democratic state. This deficiency is, as I have been saying, the enfeeblement and virtual paralysis of the executive governing functions. The strong medicine of the counterrevolution is needed, on the one hand, to stop the electoral process from encroaching upon and invading the government, and, on the other hand, to invest the government not only with all material power but also with the imponderable force of majesty.

It is possible to govern a state without giving the masses of the people full representation. But it is not possible to go on for long without a government which can and does in fact govern. If, therefore, the people find that they must choose whether they will be represented in an assembly which is incompetent to govern, or whether they will be governed without being represented, there is no doubt at all as to how the issue will be decided. They will choose authority, which promises to be paternal, in preference to freedom which threatens to be fratricidal. For large communities cannot do without being governed. No ideal of freedom and of democracy will long be allowed to stand in the way of their being governed.

The plight of the modern democracies is serious. They have suffered great disasters in this century and the consequences of these disasters are compounding themselves. The end is not yet clear. The world that is safe for democracy and is safely democratic is shrunken. It is still shrinking. For the disorder which has been incapacitating the democracies in this century is, if anything, becoming more virulent as time goes on.

A continuing practical failure to govern will lead—no one can say in what form and under what banners—to counterrevolutionary measures for the establishment of strong government. The alternative is to withstand and to reverse the descent towards counterrevolution. It is a much harder way. It demands popular assent to radical measures which will restore government strong enough to govern, strong enough to resist the encroachment of the assemblies and of mass opinions, and strong enough to guarantee private liberty against the pressure of the masses.

It would be foolish to attempt to predict whether the crisis of the democratic state will be resolved by such an internal restoration and revival or by counterrevolution. No doubt the danger of counterrevolution is greater in countries where the margins of life are thinner. No doubt the prospects of a restoration and revival are best in countries where the traditions of civility, as the public philosophy of Western society, have deep roots and a long history.

CHAPTER SEVEN

The Adversaries of Liberal Democracy

1. *Liberalism and Jacobinism*

WE ARE living in a time of massive popular counter-revolution agai s l'beral democr.cv It is a reaction to the failure of the West to cope with the miseries and anxieties of the Twentieth Century. The liberal democracies have been tried and found wanting—found wanting not only in their capa ity to govern success fully in this period of wars and upheavals, but also in their ability to defend and maintain the political philosophy that underlies the liberal way of life.

If we go back to the beginnings of the modern democratic movements in the eighteenth century, we can distinguish two diverging lines of development. The one is a way of progress in liberal constitutional democracy. The other is a morbid course of development into totalitarian conditions.[1]

One of the first to realize what was happening was Alexis de Tocqueville. He foresaw that the "democratic nations are menaced" by a "species of oppression . . . unlike anything that ever before existed in the world." But what is more, he discerned the original difference between the healthy and the morbid development of democracy.

In 1833, after his voyage in America, where he had foreseen the threat of mass democracy, de Tocqueville visited England.[2] There he was impressed with the contrast between the attitude of the English aristocracy,

---

[1] Cf. J. C. Talmon, *The Rise of Totalitarian Democracy*.

[2] De Tocqueville did not write a book on England, as he had already written one on America and was later to write one on France. His views on England were not accessible until recently, when Miss Ada Zemach published her study, *Alexis de Tocqueville on England*, in the *Review of Politics* for July 1951, Vol. 13, No. 3. This valuable paper is collated from de Tocqueville's correspondence and notes. Miss Zemach says that "unlike his views on Amer-

which was just in the way of accommodating itself to a newly enfranchised mass of voters, and the French *noblesse* of the *Ancien Régime*.

He went on to reflect that

> . . . from an early time a fundamental difference existed between the behavior of the governing classes in England and in France. The nobility, the cornerstone of medieval society, revealed in England a peculiar ability to merge and mix with other social groups, while in France it tended, on the contrary, to close its ranks and preserve its original purity of birth.

> In the earlier Middle Ages all Western Europe had a similar social system. But some time in the Middle Ages, one cannot say exactly when, a change pregnant with tremendous consequences occurred in the British Isles and in the British Isles only—the English nobility developed into an open aristocracy while the continental *noblesse* stubbornly remained within the rigid limits of a caste.

This, observes de Tocqueville, is the most revolutionary fact in English history, and he claims to have been the first to observe its importance and to grasp its full significance. It is, truly, a deep and illuminating observation on the conditions which are favorable to a healthy and progressive evolution of democracy and on the conditions whch make it morbid and degenerative. The crucial difference is between what we might call enfranchisement by assimilation into the governing class, as exemplified in England, and, *per contra,* enfranchisement by the overthrow and displacing of the governing class as exemplified in France. In the one the government remains but becomes more responsible and more responsive; in the other, the government is overthrown with the liquidation of the governing class.

Although the two ways of evolution appear to have the same object—a society with free institutions under popu-

ica and France, which are carefully stated in special books written at great length and in elaborate form, his ideas about England are more impressionistic in nature, scattered as they are in no particular order among volumes of correspondence, sometimes appearing in a bunch in the *Journal de Voyage,* sometimes as sudden asides in the big systematic works, emphasizing and defining a certain trend of thought by way of comparison and opposition."

lar government—they are radically different and they arrive at radically different ends.

The first way, that of assimilation, presumes the existence of a state which is already constitutional in principle, which is under laws that are no longer arbitrary, though they may be unjust and unequal. Into this constitutional state more and more people are admitted to the governing class and to the voting electorate. The unequal and the unjust laws are revised until eventually all the people have equal opportunities to enter the government and to be represented. Broadly speaking, this has been the working theory of the British movement towards a democratic society at home and also in the Commonwealth and Empire. This, too, was the working theory of the principal authors of the American Constitution, and this was how —though few of them welcomed it—they envisaged the enfranchisement of the whole adult population.

The other way is that of the Jacobin revolution. The people rise to power by overthrowing the ruling class and by liquidating its privileges and prerogatives. This is the doctrine of democratic revolution which was developed by French thinkers in the eighteenth century and was put into practice by the Jacobin party in the French Revolution. In its English incarnation the doctrine became known as Radicalism. In America, though it had its early disciples, notably Tom Paine, not until the era of the Founding Fathers was over, not until the era of Andrew Jackson, did the Jacobin doctrine become the popular political creed of the American democracy.

The Jacobin philosophy rests on a view of human society which the encyclopedist, Holbach, stated in this way:

> We see on the face of the globe only incapable, unjust sovereigns, enervated by luxury, corrupted by flattery, depraved through unpunished license, and without talent, morals, or good qualities.[3]

What Holbach had, in fact, seen on the face of the globe was the French court—then the most powerful in Europe and the paragon of all the lesser courts. When he was writing, it would have been difficult for anyone on the continent of Europe to imagine a king and a ruling class

[3] Cited in Hippolyte A. Taine, *The Ancient Régime* (1888), p. 220.

who were not, like those he saw living at the Court of Versailles, exclusive and incompetent, corrupt, unteachable and unconcerned.

"Would you know the story in brief, of almost all our wretchedness?" asked Diderot. "Here it is. There existed the natural man, and into this man was introduced an artificial man, whereupon a civil war arose within him lasting through life . . . If you propose to become a tyrant over him, . . . do your best to poison him with a theory of morals against nature; impose every kind of fetter on him; embarrass his movements with a thousand obstacles; place phantoms around him to frighten him. Would you see him happy and free? Do not meddle with his affairs. . . . I appeal to every civil, religious and political institution; examine these closely, and, if I am not mistaken, you will find the human species, century after century, subject to a yoke which a mere handful of knaves chose to impose on it. . . . Be wary of him who seeks to establish order; to order is to obtain the mastery of others by giving them trouble.[4]

If we compare the mood of this passage with that of the Declaration of Independence, the work of the other brand of revolutionists, we must be struck by the nihilism of Diderot. Diderot had been exasperated to a blind destructive despair by the rigidity of the French governing caste. He could not feel that there was anything to be done with any government, judging by the one he suffered under, except to abolish it.

Jefferson and his colleagues, on the other hand, were interested in government. They were in rebellion because they were being denied the rights of representation and of participation which they, like other subjects of the same King, would have enjoyed had they lived in England. The Americans were in rebellion against the "usurpations" of George III, not against authority as such but against the abuse of authority. The American revolutionists had in fact participated in the colonial governments. They intended to play leading parts, as indeed they did, in the new government. Far from wishing to overthrow the authority of government, or to deny and subvert, as Diderot did, the moral foundations of authority, they went into rebellion

[4] *Ibid.*, pp. 220-221.

first in order to gain admittance into, and then to take possession of, the organs of government.

When they declared that "a prince (George III) whose character is thus marked by every act which may define a tyrant, is unfit to be the ruler of a free people," they were not saying that there was *no one* who was fit to be the ruler of a free people. They were imbued with the English idea that the governing class must learn to share its special prerogatives by admitting new members. The American Revolutionists were themselves the new members who had been unjustly, in fact illegally, excluded from the government of the colonies. They themselves meant to govern the colonies after they had overthrown the government of the King. They were not nihilists to whom the revolutionary act of overthrowing the sovereign is the climax and consummation of everything.

2. *The Paradigm of Revolution*

OF THE two rival philosophies, the Jacobin is almost everywhere in the ascendant. It is a ready philosophy for men who, previously excluded from the ruling class, and recently enfranchised, have no part in the business of governing the state, and no personal expectation of being called upon to assume the responsibilities of office. The Jacobin doctrine is an obvious reaction, as de Tocqueville's observation explains, to government by a caste. When there is no opening for the gradualness of reform and for enfranchisement by assimilation, a revolutionary collision is most likely.

The Jacobin doctrine is addressed to the revolutionary collision between the inviolable governing caste and the excluded men claiming the redress of their grievances and their place in the sun. Though it professes to be a political philosophy, the doctrine is not, in fact, a philosophy of government. It is a gospel and also a strategy for revolution. It announces the promise that the crusade which is to overthrow the ruling caste will by the act of revolution create a good society.

The peculiar essence of the dogma is that the revolution itself is the creative act. Towards the revolution as such, because it is the culmination and the climax, all the labor and the sacrifice of the struggle are to be directed. The revolutionary act will remove the causes of evil in human society. Again and again it has been proved how effective is this formula for arousing, sustaining and organizing men's energies for revolution: to declare that evil in society has been imposed upon the many by the few—by priests, nobles, capitalists, imperialists, liberals, aliens—and that evil will disappear when the many who are pure have removed these few who are evil.

The summons to revolution in the *Communist Manifesto* of 1848 uses the same formula as the Jacobins had used a half century earlier. Marx and Engels were men steeped in the Western revolutionary tradition, and habituated, therefore, to the notion that the act of revolution removes the source of evil and creates the perfect society. The French Revolution had not made this perfect society. For by 1848 there were the capitalist oppressors. Marx and Engels called for the next revolutionary act, announcing that now the Third Estate, the bourgeois capitalists, needed to go the way of the liquidated nobles and clergy.

This is the formula: that when the revolution of the masses is victorious over the few, there will exist the classless society without coercion and violence and with freedom for all. This formula reappears whenever conditions are revolutionary—that is to say, when necessary reforms are being refused. The formula is the strategy of rebellion of those who are unable to obtain the redress of grievances. The rulers are to be attacked. So they are isolated. They are few. So they are not invincible. They bear the total guilt of all the sufferings and grievances of men. To remove them is then to cure all evil. Therefore, their overthrow, which is feasible, will be worth every sacrifice. Since the world will be good when the evil few have been overthrown, there is no need for the doubts and the disputes which would arise among the revolutionists if they had to make serious practical decisions on the problems of the post-revolutionary world.

"You are summoned," said Barrère to the National Assembly, "to give history a fresh start." [5] This was to be done by stripping off, as Taine puts it the garments of the artificial man, all those fictitious qualities which make him "ecclesiastic or layman, noble or plebeian, sovereign or subject, proprietor or proletarian, ignorant or cultivated." The established authorities who have made man wear these garments for their selfish and sinister ends must go. The

[5] *Ibid.*, p. 232.

authorities must go, the garments must be removed, and then there will be left "man in himself, the same under all conditions, in all situations, in all countries, in all ages."

These natural men would be very different from the fallen and deformed wretches who now inhabit the world. They would be Adam before he fell—Adam who fell by the machinations of the tyrants and the priests, and not by his own disobedience. Let this "infamous thing," with its upholders, be crushed, said Voltaire of the *ancien régime*. Then, added Condorcet exultingly, "tyrants and slaves, and priests with their senseless and hypocritical instruments," will disappear, and there will be only "free men recognizing no other master than reason." [6]

To appreciate the compelling influence of these ideas, we must realize that Rousseau and his Jacobin disciples were not saying that "except for the clergy and the nobility" all the Frenchmen of the eighteenth century were rational and good men. That may have been what the most simple-minded got from the Jacobin orations. But the doctrine could never have become, as in fact it has, the political religion of the democracies had it stood for anything so obviously contrary to common sense and ordinary experience.

Rousseau's dogma of the natural goodness of man did not move him to much love or admiration of his fellow-men. In his *Inequalities Among Mankind*, he described the inside of a civilized man in terms which John Adams, for all his tough-mindedness, found "too black and horrible to be transcribed." [7]

To Rousseau, as to John Calvin who lived in Geneva before him, men were fallen and depraved, deformed with their lusts and their aggressions. The force of the new doctrine lay in its being a gospel of redemption and regeneration. Men who were evil were to be made good. Jacobinism is, in fact, a Christian heresy—perhaps the most influential since the Arian.

In that it preached the need of redemption, its reception was prepared by the Christian education of the people of Western Europe and of North America. Like Saint Paul, the Jacobins promised a new creature who would

⁶ *Ibid.*, p. 231.

⁷ John Adams, *A Defense of the Constitutions of Government of the United States of America* (1787), from the *Life and Works of John Adams* (edited with *The Life* by Charles Francis Adams, 1851), Vol. IV., p. 409.

"be led of the spirit" and would not be "under the law." But in the Jacobin gospel, this transformation was to be achieved by the revolutionary act of emancipation from authority. The religious end was to be reached, but without undergoing the religious experience. There was to be no dark night of the soul for each person in the labor of his own regeneration. Instead there were to be riots and strikes and votes and seizure of political power. Instead of the inner struggle of the individual soul, there was to be one great public massive, collective redemption.

3. Democratic Education

WE LIVE long enough after the new gospel was proclaimed to have seen what came of it. The post-revolutionary man, enfranchised and emancipated, has not turned out to be the New Man. He is the old Adam. Yet the future of democratic society has been staked on the promises and the predictions of the Jacobin gospel.

For the Jacobin doctrine has pervaded the theory of mass education in the newly enfranchised mass democracies. In America and in most of the newer liberal democracies of the Western world, the Jacobin heresy is, though not unchallenged and not universal, the popular and dominant theory in the schools.

Its popularity is easily accounted for. It promises to solve the problem which is otherwise so nearly insoluble —how to educate rapidly and sufficiently the ever-expanding masses who are losing contact with the traditions of Western society. The explosive increase of the population in the past hundred and fifty years, its recent enfranchisement during the past fifty years, the dissolution, or at least the radical weakening, of the bonds of the family, the churches, and of the local community have combined to make the demand upon the schools almost impossibly big.

Not only do the schools have to teach the arts and sciences to a multiplying mass of pupils. They have also to act in the place of the family, the household economy, the church, and the settled community, and to be the bearers of the traditions and the disciplines of a civilized life. What the school system could do has never been anywhere nearly equal to the demands upon it. The modern democracies have never been willing to pay the price of recruiting and training enough teachers, of supporting enough schools and colleges, of offering enough scholarships to give all children equal opportunities.

The Jacobin doctrine does not solve this problem of mass education—as it does not solve or even throw light upon the problem of how to construct and govern the utopian society which is to exist when the revolution has taken place. What it does is to provide an escape from these unsolved problems. It affirms that in politics the state will wither away and then there will be no problems of how to govern it. For the democratic schools it affirms that there is no problem of supplying the demand: for almost nothing has to be taught in school and almost no effort is needed to learn it.

"The fundamental principle of all morality," said Rousseau in his reply to Archbishop de Beaumont's condemnation of his book, *Emile,* "is that man is a being naturally good, loving justice and order: that there is not any original perversity in the human heart, and that the first movements of nature are always right." [8]

And so, when Rousseau's disciple, Pestalozzi, the celebrated educator. said that "in the newborn child are hidden those faculties which are to unfold during life," [9] he meant that the hidden faculties which would unfold were all of them good ones. Only good faculties, it transpired, were inherited. The evil faculties, on the contrary, were acquired. So Froebel. who was Pestalozzi's disciple, felt able to say that "the still young being, even though as yet unconsciously like a product of nature, precisely and surely wills that which is best for himself." [10]

Froebel, of course, had no way of proving that infants are precise and sure about anything. Nor did Rousseau know how to prove that there is no perversity in the human heart, and that the first movements of nature are always right. But if only all this could be taken as true, how miraculously it simplified the problems of the new democracies! If men do not have to acquire painfully by learning, if they are born with the necessary good faculties, if their first intentions are always right, if they un-

[8] J. J. Rousseau, "Lettre à C. de Beaumont," in *Oeuvres Complètes de J. J. Rousseau,* edited by P. R. Auguis (Paris, Dalibon, 1824-1825), Vol. 7, p. 44. Translation from Geoffrey O'Connell, *Naturalism in American Education* (1938), p. 23.

[9] J. H. Pestalozzi, address on his birthday in 1818, cited in the *Encyclopedia of Religion and Ethics,* Vol. V, p. 166.

[10] F. W. A. Froebel, *Education of Man,* Sec. 8.

consciously but precisely and surely will what is best for themselves from infancy on, then there is in the very nature of things a guarantee that popular government must succeed.

The best government will be the one which governs the least and requires, therefore, the least training and experience in the art of governing. The best education for democracy will be the one which trains, disciplines, and teaches the least. For the necessary faculties are inborn and they are more likely to be perverted by too much culture than to wither for the lack of it. There is, moreover, no body of public knowledge and no public philosophy that the schools are called upon to transmit. There are, therefore, no inconvenient questions of faith and morals, questions on which there is no prospect of agreement by popular decision. The curriculum can be emptied of all the studies and the disciplines which relate to faith and to morals. And so while education can do something to enable the individual to make a success of his own career, the instinctive rightness and righteousness of the people can be relied upon for everything else.

This is a convenient and agreeably plausible escape from reality. Pestalozzi described it by saying that . . .

> Sound Education stands before me symbolized by a tree planted near fertilizing water. A little seed, which contains the design of the tree, its forms and proportion, is placed in the soil. See how it germinates and expands into trunk, branches, leaves, flowers and fruit! The whole tree is an uninterrupted chain of organic parts, the plan of which existed in its seed and root. Man is similar to the tree. In the newborn child are hidden those faculties which are to unfold during life.[11]

The metaphor reveals very neatly how the Jacobin theory inhibits education. In no way that is relevant to the problems of politics and education is a man similar, as Pestalozzi says he is, to a tree which is planted near fertilizing water. For the tree will never, no matter how fertilizing the water near which it is planted, grow up and take to writing treatises, as Pestalozzi did, on the education of trees and how to raise the best trees from all the little saplings. The tree will never worry about whether its little saplings are going to be planted near the most

[11] *Encyclopedia of Religion and Ethics,* Vol. V, p. 166.

fertilizing of the waters. The educator of a tree is, in short, not another tree. The educator of a tree, the man who plants it near the fertilizing water, is a being so radically different from a tree that the tree is incapable of being aware of his existence. If, however, the tree were enough like a man to notice such things, the teacher of the trees who cultivates them would be worshiped as the god of trees.

Pestalozzi's trees are, in fact, a caricature, but a telling one, of the educational vacuum created by the Jacobin theory. The tradition of the trees is transmitted in their seed, and the older trees are unable to teach and the saplings are unable to learn. Each tree exists for itself, drawing what it can from the fertilizing waters if they happen to be there. Now if human education is founded upon this notion, it must fail to transmit the moral system, indeed the psychic structure, of a civilized society. Relying upon the inherent rightness of the natural impulses of man's first nature, the Jacobin theory does away with the second civilized nature, with the ruler of the impulses, who is identified with the grand necessities of the commonwealth. It overthrows the ruler within each man,—he who exercises "the royal and politic rule" over his "irascible and concupiscible powers."

When reason no longer represents society within the human psyche, then it becomes the instrument of appetite, desire and passion. As William Godwin said in 1798: "Reason is wholly confined to adjusting the comparison between the different objects of desire and investigating the most successful mode of attaining those objects." [12] More than a hundred years later (1911) Prof. William MacDougal put it this way: "The instinctive impulses determine the *end* of all activities, and . . . all the complex intellectual apparatus of the most highly developed mind *is but* . . . the instrument by which those impulses seek their satisfactions. . . ." [13] Or, as Bernard Shaw has it, "Ability to reason accurately is as desirable as ever, since it is only by accurate reasoning that we can calculate our actions so as to do what we intend to do—that is, to fulfill our will." [14]

[12] From a memorandum setting forth his intended work. Reproduced in C. K. Paul, *William Godwin: His Friends and Contemporaries*. (Boston, 1876), Vol. I, p. 294.

[13] William MacDougal, *Social Psychology* (London, Methuen & Co., 1950), p. 38.

[14] G. B. Shaw, *Quintessence of Ibsenism* (1891), p. 15.

If it is the role of reason merely to be an instrument of each man's career, then the mission of the schools is to turn out efficient careerists. They must teach the know-how of success, and this—seasoned with the social amenities and some civic and patriotic exhortation—is the subject matter of education. The student elects those subjects which will presumably equip him for success in his career. The rest are superfluous. There is no such thing as a general order of knowledge and a public philosophy, which he needs to possess.

4. *From Jacobinism to Leninism*

TOWARDS the middle of the nineteenth century, Karl Marx and Friedrich Engels produced an explanation of why the first revolution had not fulfilled the promises of the Jacobins. It was that "Modern bourgeois society, rising out of the ruins of feudal society, did not make an end of class antagonisms. It merely set up new classes in place of the old."

As Marx and Engels were scholars and men of the world, they should not have been surprised to find that "the history of all human society past and present has been the history of class struggles," and, had they not become possessed by the Jacobin dogma, they would have thought it most probable that there would be class struggles in the future. But in the Jacobin philosophy the world as it is must be transformed; the day is soon to come when history, reaching its culmination, will end, and there will be no more struggles. So Marx and Engels decided that one more, though this time the conclusive and the final, revolution was called for, in order to achieve the classless society: "The proletariat . . . is compelled to organize itself as a class," and "by means of a revolution, it makes itself the ruling class and, as such, sweeps away by force the old conditions of production. . . . Then it will, along with these conditions, have swept away the conditions for the existence of class antagonisms and of classes generally, and will thereby have abolished its own supremacy as a class."

The revolution which is behind us has failed. But the revolution which is still to come will put "in place of the old bourgeois society, with its classes and class antagonisms

. . . an association, in which the free development of each is the condition of the free development of all." [15]

By the beginning of the twentieth century it was becoming more and more apparent that Marxism was going to undergo the same disappointment as had the Jacobin movement. Since Marx and Engels wrote the Communist Manifesto a very considerable progress had been made in carrying out its specific planks. What that document had asked in 1848, "the most advanced nations" had gone a long way toward doing. They were taxing inheritances, they had virtually nationalized central banking, transportation and communications, they were extending the industries owned by the state, they were abolishing child labor and providing free education in public schools. [16]

Yet these reforms were not leading to the classless society. Instead of one class or no class it was more probable that modern societies were heading towards a diversity of classes. Nor, as Engels had promised in his "Anti-Dühring," did it look as if "the state . . . withers away." As a matter of fact the progressive reforms were requiring a rapid enlargement of the powers of the state and an expansion of the bureaucracy. The Marxian predictions were not being fulfilled. The rich were not becoming richer while the poor became poorer. The middle class was not disappearing. It was growing larger. Society was not splitting into the two great hostile camps of the bourgeoisie and the proletariat. If it was splitting, it was into factions and into pressure groups.

Owing to the wide disparity between the dogma and the existential reality of things, a crisis developed within the revolutionary socialist movement. This crisis was resolved by Lenin. He could not do again what Marx had done a half century earlier. He could not once more identify the next class, and this time the positively last class, that had to be overthrown. He could not point to the last barricade that had to be stormed. It was then that Lenin resolved the crisis within the revolutionary movement by committing it to the totalitarian solution. Abandoning the naïve but attractive promise that utopia would follow simply and automatically from the revolutionary

[15] These quotations are from the Manifesto of the Communist Party (1848).
[16] Cf. the concrete proposals contained in the Communist Manifesto.

act, he replaced it with the terrible doctrine that utopia must be brought about by an i[...]ly prolonged process of un[...] revolution which would exterminate all opposition, actual and potential.

The totalitarian tendency has always been present and logically imp[...]d in the modern revolutionary movement.[17] Yet Mr. Isaiah Berlin is no doubt right in saying that while Lenin's solution of the crisis within the revolutionary movement "marked the culmination of a process," this was "an event . . . which altered the history of our world." [18]

In 1903, at the conference of the Russian Social Democratic Party, which began in Brussels and ended in London, Lenin was asked by a delegate named P[...]dovsky "whether the emphasis laid by the 'hard' Socialists . . . upon the need for the exercise of absolute authority by the revolutionary nucleus of the Party might not prove incompatible with those fundamental liberties to whose realization Socialism, no less than liberalism, was officially dedicated." Posadovsky asked whether the basic, minimum civil liberties—"the sacrosanctity of the person"—could be infringed and even violated if the party later so decided.

The answer was given by Plekhanov, one of the founders of Russian Marxism, and, says Mr. Berlin, "its most venerated figure, a cultivated, fastidious and morally sensitive scholar of wide outlook," who had for twenty years lived in Western Europe and was much respected by the leaders of Western Socialism. Plekhanov was the very symbol of civilized "scientific" thinking among Russian revolutionaries. "Plekhanov, speaking solemnly, and with a splendid disregard for grammar, pronounced the words, *salus revolutiae suprema lex*. Certainly, if the revolution demanded it, everything—democracy, liberty, the rights of the individual—must be sacrificed to it. If the democratic assembly elected by the Russian people after the revolution proved amenable to Marxist tactics, it would be kept in being as a Long Parliament: if not it would be disbanded as quickly as possible. A Marxist revolution could not be carried through by men obsessed by scrupulous regard for the principles of bourgeois liberals. Doubtless

[17] Cf. Eric Voegelin, *The New Science of Politics,* particularly Ch. IV, et seq.; also J. L. Talmon, *The Rise of Totalitarian Democracy*.

[18] Isaiah Berlin, "Political Ideas in the Twentieth Century" (*Foreign Affairs,* April 1950, Vol. XXVIII, No. 3, pp. 364-366).

whatever was valuable in these principles, like everything else good and desirable, would ultimately be realized by the victorious working class; but during the revolutionary period preoccupation with such ideals was evidence of a lack of seriousness."

Mr. Berlin goes on to say that "Plekhanov, who was brought up in a humane and liberal tradition, did, of course, later retreat from this position himself. The mixture of utopian faith and brutal disregard for civilized morality proved too repulsive to a man who had spent the greater part of his civilized and productive life among Western workers and their leaders. Like the vast majority of Social Democrats, like Marx and Engels themselves, he was too European to try to realize a policy which, in the words of Shigalev in Dostoevski's *The Possessed,* 'starting from unlimited liberty ends in unlimited despotism.' But Lenin accepted the premises, and being logically driven to conclusions repulsive to most of his colleagues, accepted them easily and without apparent qualms. His assumptions were, perhaps, in some sense, still those of the optimistic rationalists of the eighteenth and nineteenth centuries: the coercion, violence, execution, the total suppression of individual differences, the rule of a small, virtually self-appointed minority, were necessary only in the interim period, only so long as there was a powerful enemy to be destroyed."

But how was it that Lenin, and so many after him, have accepted easily and without apparent qualms the repulsive process of violence, executions, suppressions, deception, under the unlimited rule of self-appointed oligarchs? Why do the full-fledged totalitarians, Lenin, Hitler, Stalin, not shrink from the means they adopt to achieve their end? The answer is that the inhuman means are justified by the superhuman end: they are the agents of history or of nature. They are the men appointed to fulfill the destiny of creation. They have been known as atheists. But in fact God was their enemy, not because they did not believe in the Deity, but because they themselves were assuming His functions and claiming His prerogatives.

5. *The Overpassing of the Bound*

THIS IS the root of the matter, and it is here that the ultimate issue lies. Can men, acting like gods, be appointed to establish heaven on earth? If we believe that they can be, then the rest follows. To fulfill their mission they must assume a godlike omnipotence. They must be jealous gods, monopolizing power, destroying all rivals, compelling exclusive loyalty. The family, the churches, the schools, the corporations, the labor unions and co-operative societies, the voluntary associations and all the arts and sciences, must be their servants. Dissent and deviation are treason and quietism is sacrilege.

But the monopoly of all power will not be enough. There remains the old Adam. Unless they can remake the fallen nature of a man, the self-elected gods cannot make a heaven of the earth. In the Jacobin gospel of the eighteenth century, and even in the Marxist gospel of the nineteenth century, the new man would be there when the artificial garments were removed—when once he was emancipated by the revolutionary act from the deformation imposed upon him by the clergy, the nobility and the bourgeoisie. A hundred years later the new man was nowhere in sight. So the early and softer gospel gave way to a later and infinitely harder one. The new man and the new heaven on earth demanded the remaking of pre-Leninist and pre-Hitlerian man. The decrees of history as revealed to Marx, and the decrees of nature as revealed to Hitler, had to be carried out.

But in order to do that, the human species had first to be transformed—or failing that, exterminated. Destiny called upon the mortal god to make surviving mankind "an active unfailing carrier," as Hannah Arendt says, "of a law to which human beings would otherwise only passively and reluctantly be subject." [19]

In the eyes of its devotees, this is not an inhuman and satanic doctrine. It is above and beyond humanity. It is for the superman that its gospel announces. The ruthlessness, the arbitrariness, the cruelty are not monstrous

---

[19] Hannah Arendt, *Ideology and Terror; A Novel Form of Government.* From the *Review of Politics* (published at the University of Notre Dame, July, 1953), Vol. XV, No. 3.

wickedness. They are natural and necessary, predestined like the fall of a sparrow, in the sublime construction of the earthly paradise.

The issue is carried outside the realm of rational discourse. As Richard Hooker said of the Puritan revolutionaries three centuries ago, when men believe they are acting "under the absolute command of Almighty God," their discipline "must be received . . . although the world by receiving it should be clean turned upside down." [20] There is no arguing with the pretenders to a divine knowledge and to a divine mission. They are possessed with the sin of pride, they have yielded to the perennial temptation. This is the sovereign evil against which the traditions of civility are arrayed.

Here is "the mortal sin original," the forbidden fruit, which Satan tempts Eve to eat:

Taste this, and be henceforth among the Gods Thyself
a Goddess.[21]

This tasting of the tree, as Adam says to Dante, was "the overpassing of the bound." [22]

Zeus, says Aeschylus

. . . is a chastener of froward wills
And he correcteth with a heavy hand.
Wherefore be ye instructors of your Lord,
And with well-reasoned admonitions teach Him
To have a humbler heart and cast away
The sin of pride, for it offendeth God.[23]

The delusion of men that they are gods—the pretension that they have a commission to act as if they were gods—is, says Aeschylus, "the blind arrogance of childish thought." It can become "the very madness of a mind diseased." Yet it is not a new and recent infection, but rather the disposition of our first natures, of our natural

[20] *Of the Laws of Ecclesiastical Polity*. In Vol. I, *The Works of Richard Hooker*, edited by J. Keble (second edition, Oxford University, 1841), Preface, Ch. VIII, Sec. 5, p. 182.
[21] *Paradise Lost*. In *The Poetical Works of John Milton*, Bk. V, lines 77-78.
[22] *Divine Comedy*, translated by C. E. Norton (1941), *Paradise*, Canto XXVI, verse 117.
[23] *The Persians*, lines 828-836.

and uncivilized selves. Men have been barbarians much longer than they have been civilized. They are only precariously civilized, and within us there is the propensity, persistent as the force of gravity, to revert under stress and strain, under neglect or temptation. to our first natures.

Rousseau and the Jacobins, Marx and the nineteenth-century socialists, id not introduce new impulses and passions into men. They exploited and varied impulses and passions that are always there. 1 the traditions of civility, man's second and more rational nature must master his first and more elemental.

The Jacobins and their successors made a political religion founded up n the reversal of civility. Instead of ruling the elemental impulses, they stimulated and armed them. Instead of treating he present n to being a god as the mortal sin original, they proclaimed it to be the glory and destiny of man. Upon this ground they founded a popular religion of the rise of the to power. Lenin, Hitler and Stalin, the hard totalitarian Jacobins of the twentieth century, carried this movement and the logical implications of its gospel further and further towards the very bitter end.

And what is that bitter end? It is an everlasting war with the human condition: war with he finitude of man and with the moral ends of finite man. and, therefore, war against freedom, against justice, against the laws and against the order of the good society—as they are conserved in the traditions of civility, as they are articulated in the public philosophy.

BOOK TWO

The Public Philosophy

CHAPTER EIGHT

The Eclipse of the Public Philosophy

1. On the Efficacy of Ideas

THERE are those who would say, using the words of philosophers to prove it, that it is the characteristic illusion of the tender-minded that they believe in philosophy. Those who can, do; those who cannot, teach and theorize. And being theorists by profession, they exaggerate the efficacy of ideas, which are mere airy nothings without mass or energy, the mere shadows of the existential world of substance and of force, of habits and desires, of machines and armies.

Yet the illusion, if it were one, is inordinately tenacious. It is impossible to remove it from the common sense in which we live and have our being. In the familiar daylight world we cannot act as if ideas had no consequences. The whole vast labor and passion of public life would be nonsense if we did not believe that it makes a difference what is done by parties, newspapers, books, broadcasts, schools and churches. All their effort would be irrelevant, indeed nonsense, like an argument about what Nebuchadnezzar should be served for tomorrow morning's breakfast.

The most thoroughgoing skeptic is unable, in practice, to make a clean sweep—to say that since ideas have no consequences there is no such thing as a good idea or a bad one, a true idea or a false one. For there is no escaping the indubitable fact of experience that we are often mistaken, and that it makes a difference to have been wrong.

The chemistry of our bodies is never mistaken. The reaction of one chemical element to another chemical element is always correct, is never misled by misinformation, by untruth, and by illusion. The doctor can be mistaken about the chemistry of his patient, having failed to detect a substance which falsifies his diagnosis. But it is only the doctor who can be wrong; the chemical process cannot be.

Why do men make mistakes? Because an important part of human behavior is reaction to the pictures in their heads. Human behavior takes place in relation to a pseudo-environment—a representation, which is not quite the same for any two individuals, of what they suppose to be —not what *is*—the reality of things.[1] This man-made, this cultural environment, which has its being in the minds of men, is interposed between man as a biological organism and the external reality. It is in this realm that ideas are efficacious. They are efficacious because men react to their ideas and images, to their pictures and notions of the world, treating these pictures as if they were the reality.

The airy nothings in the realm of essence are efficacious in the existential world when a man, believing it to be true or good, treats the idea as if it were the reality. In this way faith in an idea can quite literally remove a mountain. To be sure no man's idea can remove a mountain on the moon. But if the American people took it into their heads that life would not be worth living until Pike's Peak was in the suburbs of Chicago, they could move Pike's Peak. They could do it if they and their descendants were sufficiently devoted to the idea for a long enough time.

Nothing would happen to Pike's Peak if the idea of removing it were merely proclaimed and celebrated. The idea would have to become, like the idea of winning a war, the object and the focus of the nation's energies. Then the idea would operate in the minds of men who voted, who planned, who would engineer the undertaking, who would raise the money, would recruit the labor, would procure the equipment, and—shall we say—would suppress the mounting resistance of the objectors to the project.

Because ideas have the power to organize human be-

[1] Cf. my *Public Opinion,* Chapters I to X.

havior, their efficacy can be radical. They are indeed radical when, as the image of what a man should be, they govern the formation of his character and so imprint a lasting organization on his behavior.[2] Because the images of man are the designs of the molds in which characters are formed, they are of critical concern. What is the image of the good king, the good courtier, the good subject— of the good master and of the good slave—of the good citizen, the good soldier, the good politician, the good boss, the good workingman? The images matter very much. The ones which prevail will govern education. The ideas of what men should be like become efficacious in the existential world because, as they are imposed by the family, the school and the community, they cause men to "acquire the kind of character which makes them *want* to act in the way they *have* to act as members of the society or of a special class within it." They learn "to *desire* what, objectively, it is necessary for them to do," and *"outer force* is . . . replaced by" the *"inner compulsion"* of their own characters.[3]

That there are limits to education in this sense, we cannot doubt. But we do not know where they are. There is, that is to say, no clear and certain boundary between character which is acquired and those more or less uneducable traits of human nature, evolved during the long ages and transmitted by inheritance. We are quite unable to predict with any certainty or precision how far the individual pupil is educable—or rather how far he is still educable by the time a particular educator gets hold of him, and after he has already acquired a character of sorts in his infancy.

Yet, however crude and clumsy our knowledge of the process, there is no doubt that a character is acquired by experience and education. Within limits that we have not measured, human nature is malleable. Can we doubt it when we remember that when Shakespeare was alive there were no Americans, that when Virgil was alive there were

---

[2] I am using the term "character" as Erich Fromm does, in his *Man for Himself* (1947), p. 49, meaning "the relatively permanent form in which human energy is canalized in the process of assimilation and socialization."

[3] Erich Fromm, "Individual and Social Origin of Neurosis," *American Sociological Review*, Vol. 9 (1944), pp. 380-384. Reprinted in Clyde Kluckhohn and Henry Alexander Murray, *Personality in Nature, Society, and Culture*, (1948), pp. 407, *et seq.*

no Englishmen, and that when Homer was alive there were no Romans? Quite certainly, men have acquired the ways of thinking, feeling and acting which we recognize as their ethnic, national, class and occupational characteristics. Comparatively speaking these characteristics are, moreover, recently acquired. Even within the brief span of historical time characters have been acquired and have been lost and have been replaced by other characters. This is what gives to man's history, despite his common humanity, its infinite variety.

Because human nature is, as Hocking puts it, "the most plastic part of the living world, the most adaptable, the most educable,"[4] it is also the most mal-adaptable and mis-educable. The cultural heritage which contains the whole structure and fabric of the good life is acquired. It may be rejected. It may be acquired badly. It may not be acquired at all. For we are not born with it. If it is not transmitted from one generation to the next, it may be lost, indeed forgotten through a dark age, until somewhere and somehow men rediscover it, and, exploring the world again, recreate it anew.

The acquired culture is not transmitted in our genes, and so the issue is always in doubt. The good life in the good society, though attainable, is never attained and possessed once and for all. So what has been attained will again be lost if the wisdom of the good life in a good society is not transmitted.

That is the central and critical condition of the Western society: that the democracies are ceasing to receive the traditions of civility in which the good society, the liberal, democratic way of life at its best, originated and developed. They are cut off from the public philosophy and the political arts which are needed to govern the liberal democratic society. They have not been initiated into its secrets, and they do not greatly care for as much of it as they are prepared to understand.

In Toynbee's terrible phrase, they are proletarians who are "in" but are not "of" the society they dominate.

[4] William Ernest Hocking, *Human Nature and Its Remaking* (1923), p. 15.

2. *The Great Vacuum*

To SPEAK of a public philosophy is, I am well aware, to raise dangerous questions, rather like opening Pandora's box.

Within the Western nations, as Father Murray has put it, there is "a plurality of incompatible faiths";[5] there is also a multitude of secularized and agnostic people. Since there is so little prospect of agreement, and such certainty of dissension, on the content of the public philosophy, it seems expedient not to raise the issues by talking about them. It is easier to follow the rule that each person's beliefs are private and that only overt conduct is a public matter.

One might say that this prudent rule reflects and registers the terms of settlement of the religious wars and of the long struggle against exclusive authority in the realm of the spirit by "thrones or dominations, or principalities or powers."

Freedom of religion and of thought and of speech were achieved by denying both to the state and to the established church a sovereign monopoly in the field of religion, philosophy, morals, science, learning, opinion and conscience. The liberal constitutions, with their bills of rights, fixed the boundaries past which the sovereign—the King, the Parliament, the Congress, the voters—were forbidden to go.

Yet the men of the seventeenth and eighteenth centuries who established these great salutary rules would certainly have denied that a community could do without a general public philosophy. They were themselves the adherents of a public philosophy—of the doctrine of natural law, which held that there was law "above the ruler and the sovereign people . . . above the whole community of mortals."[6]

The traditions of civility spring from this principle,

[5] John Courtney Murray, S.J., "The Problem of Pluralism in America," in *Thought* (Fordham University, Summer, 1954).

[6] Cf. Otto von Gierke, *Political Theories of the Middle Age*, translated with an introduction by Frederick William Maitland (London, Cambridge University Press, 1927), pp. 73-87; and more especially note #256. Also cf. Leo Strauss, *Natural Right and History* (1953).

which was first worked out by the Stoics. As Ernest Barker says:

> The rational faculty of man was conceived as producing a common conception of law and order which possessed a universal validity. . . . This common conception included, as its three great notes, the three values of Liberty, Equality and the brotherhood or Fraternity of all mankind. This common conception, and its three great notes, have formed a European set of ideas for over two thousand years. It was a set of ideas which lived and moved in the Middle Ages; and St. Thomas Aquinas cherished the idea of a sovereign law of nature imprinted in the heart and nature of man, to which kings and legislators must everywhere bow. It was a set of ideas which lived and acted with an even greater animation from the days of the Reformation to those of the French Revolution . . . Spoken through the mouth of Locke, [they had justified] the English Revolution of 1688, and had recently served to inspire the American Revolution of 1776 . . . They were ideas of the proper conduct of states and governments in the area of internal affairs. They were ideas of the natural rights of man—of liberty, political and civic, with sovereignty residing essentially in the nation, and with free communication of thoughts and opinions; of equality before the law, and the equal repartition of public expenses among all the members of the public; of a general fraternity which tended in practice to be sadly restricted within the nation, but which could, on occasion, be extended by decree to protect all nations struggling for freedom.[7]

These traditions were expounded in the treatises of philosophers, were developed in the tracts of the publicists, were absorbed by the lawyers and applied in the courts. At times of great stress some of the endangered traditions were committed to writing, as in the Magna Carta and the Declaration of Independence. For the guidance of judges and lawyers, large portions were described—as in Lord Coke's examination of the common law. The public philosophy was in part expounded in the Bill of Rights of 1689. It was re-enacted in the first ten amendments of the

---

[7] Sir Ernest Barker, *Traditions of Civility* (1948), pp. 10-12.

Constitution of the United States. The largest part of
the public philosophy was never explicitly stated. Being
the wisdom of a great society over the generations, it can
never be stated in any single document. But the traditions
of civility permeated the peoples of the West and provided
a standard of public and private action which promoted,
facilitated and protected the institutions of freedom and
the growth of democracy.

The founders of our free institutions were themselves
adherents of this public philosophy. When they insisted
upon excluding the temporal power from the realm of
the mind and the spirit, it was not that they had no public
philosophy. It was because experience had taught them
that as power corrupts, it corrupts the public philosophy.
It was, therefore, a practical rule of politics that the government should not be given sovereignty and proprietorship
over the public philosophy.

But as time went on, there fell out of fashion the public
philosophy of the founders of Western institutions. The
rule that the temporal power should be excluded from the
realm of the mind and of the spirit was then subtly transformed. It became the rule that ideas and principles are
private—with only subjective relevance and significance.
Only when there is "a clear and present danger" to public
order are the acts of speaking and publishing in the public
domain. All the first and last things were removed from
the public domain. All that has to do with what man is
and should be, or how he should hold himself in the
scheme of things, what are his rightful ends and the legitimate means, became private and subjective and publicly
unaccountable. And so, the liberal democracies of the
West became the first great society to treat as a private
concern the formative beliefs that shape the character of
its citizens.

This has brought about a radical change in the meaning of freedom. Originally it was founded on the postulate
that there was a universal order on which all reasonable
men were agreed: within that public agreement on the
fundamentals and on the ultimates, it was safe to permit
and it would be desirable to encourage, dissent and dispute. But with the disappearance of the public philosophy
—and of a consensus on the first and last things—there
was opened up a great vacuum in the public mind, yawn-
ing to be filled.

As long as it worked, there was an obvious practical

advantage in treating the struggle for the ultimate allegiance of men as not within the sphere of the public interest. It was a way of not having to open the Pandora's box of theological, moral and ideological issues which divide the Western society. But in this century, when the hard decisions have had to be made, this rule of prudence has ceased to work. The expedient worked only as long as the general mass of the people were not seriously dissatisfied with things as they were. It was an expedient that looked towards reforms and improvement. But it assumed a society which was secure, progressive, expanding, and unchallenged. That is why it was only in the fine Victorian weather, before the storm clouds of the great wars began to gather, that the liberal democratic policy of public agnosticism and practical neutrality in ultimate issues was possible.

3. *The Neglect of the Public Philosophy*

WE COME, then, to a crucial question. If the discussion of public philosophy has been, so to speak, tabled in the liberal democracies, can we assume that, though it is not being discussed, there is a public philosophy? Is there a body of positive principles and precepts which a good citizen cannot deny or ignore? I am writing this book in the conviction that there is. It is a conviction which I have acquired gradually, not so much from a theoretical education, but rather from the practical experience of seeing how hard it is for our generation to make democracy work. I believe there is a public philosophy. Indeed there is such a thing as the public philosophy of civility. It does not have to be discovered or invented. It is known. But it does have to be revived and renewed.

The public philosophy is known as *natural law,* a name which, alas, causes great semantic confusion.[8] This philosophy is the premise of the institutions of the Western society, and they are, I believe, unworkable in communities that do not adhere to it. Except on the premises of this philosophy, it is impossible to reach intelligible and workable conceptions of popular election, majority rule,

[8] Cf. Mortimer Adler, "The Doctrine of Natural Law in Philosophy," *University of Notre Dame Natural Law Institute Proceedings,* Vol. I, pp. 65-84.

representative assemblies, free speech, loyalty, property, corporations and voluntary associations. The founders of these institutions, which the recently enfranchised democracies have inherited, were all of them adherents of some one of the various schools of natural law.

In our time the institutions built upon the foundations of the public philosophy still stand. But they are used by a public who are not being taught, and no longer adhere to, the philosophy. Increasingly, the people are alienated from the inner principles of their institutions. The question is whether and how this alienation can be overcome, and the rupture of the traditions of civility repaired.

Needless to say I am not about to argue that the rupture can be repaired by a neo-classical or neo-medieval restoration, or by some kind of romantic return to feudalism, folk-dancing and handicrafts. We cannot rub out the modern age, we cannot roll back the history that has made us what we are. We cannot start again as if there had been no advance of science, no spread of rationalism and secularism, no industrial revolution, no dissolution of the old habitual order of things, no sudden increase in the population. The poignant question is whether, and, if so, how modern men could make vital contact with the lost traditions of civility.

The appearance of things is quite obviously unpromising. There is radical novelty in our modern ways of life. The climate of feeling and the style of thought have changed radically. Modern men will first need to be convinced that the traditions of civility were not abandoned because they became antiquated. This is one of the roots of their unbelief and there is no denying its depth. Since the public philosophy preceded the advance of modern science and the industrial revolution, how can it be expected to provide a positive doctrine which is directly and practically relevant to the age we live in?

It does, one must admit, look like that, and quite evidently the original principles and precepts do not now provide the specific rules and patterns of a way of life in the circumstances of this age. A rereading of the political classics from Aristotle to Burke will not give the answers to the immediate and concrete questions: to the burning issues of diplomacy, military defense, trade, taxes, prices, and wages. Nor have the classical books anything to say about repairing automobiles, treating poliomyelitis, or proceeding with nuclear fission. As handbooks for the busy man, wanting to know how to do this or that, they are now lamentably out of date. The language is archaic, the idiom is strange, the images are unfamiliar, the practical precepts are addressed to forgotten issues.

But this irrelevance and remoteness might be the dust which has settled during the long time when philosophers and scholars and popular educators have relegated the public philosophy to the attic, when they have treated it as no longer usable by modern and progressive men. It is a neglected philosophy. For several generations it has been exceptional and indeed eccentric to use this philosophy in the practical discussion of public policies.

Neglect might well explain its dilapidated condition. If this were the explanation, it would encourage us to explore the question of a renascence. Could modern men again make vital contact with the traditions of civility? At least once before something of the sort did happen. The traditions were articulated in the Graeco-Roman world, and submerged in the West by the decline and the fall of the Western empire. Later on they were revived and renovated and remade in a great flowering of discovery and enterprise and creativity. The revival of learning did not provide maps for Columbus to use in discovering America. But it did produce much human wisdom which helped Columbus and his contemporaries to discover themselves and their possibilities.

The ancient world, we may remind ourselves, was not destroyed because the traditions were false. They were submerged, neglected, lost. For the men adhering to them had become a dwindling minority who were overthrown and displaced by men who were alien to the traditions, having never been initiated and adopted into them. May it not be that while the historical circumstances are obviously so different, something like that is happening again?

4. *The Universal Laws of the Rational Order*

FOR OVER two thousand years, says Barker, European thought has been acted upon by the idea that the rational faculties of men can produce a common conception of law and order which possesses a universal validity. This conception was first formulated as a theory by Zeno and the Stoics. It was absorbed by the Roman lawyers, was adopted by the Christian fathers, was re-established and reworked by Saint Thomas Aquinas, and in a new formulation, after the Renaissance and Reformation, it provided the philosophy of the English Revolution of 1688 and of the American Revolution of 1776. The long life of this idea and, above all, the recurring revival of the idea in all ages, would seem to indicate that it reflects a wide and recurring human need—that it is involved with practical questions of policy in the face of recurring political problems.

That the idea is not mere moonshine and cobwebs is attested by history. Barker tells us that in 330 B.C. Alexander was planning the empire in which he would be equally lord of the Greeks and the Persians, in which both Greeks and Persians would be equally bound to perform military service, and would be encouraged to intermarry. This was a revolutionary idea. Aristotle, who was then teaching at the Lyceum, advised Alexander against a policy which would bring the two worlds—the Greek and the barbarian—into the same political system. Aristotle advised Alexander to deal with the Greeks as a leader and with the Persians as a master.

But Alexander rejected the advice, certainly for practical reasons, and perhaps also for idealistic reasons. He "acted in the spirit of the policy afterwards enunciated by Eratosthenes [an Alexandrian scholar of the next century] who, 'refusing to agree with men who divided mankind into Greeks and barbarians . . . declared that it was better to divide men simply into the good and bad.'" [9]

In adopting this policy, Alexander anticipated in action what Zeno and the Stoics were soon to be teaching —that, as Plutarch wrote long afterwards, "men should not live their lives in so many civic republics, separated from one another by different systems of justice; they should reckon *all* as their fellow citizens, and there should be one life and one order *(cosmos),* as it were of one flock on a common pasture, feeding in common under one joint law." [10]

We must here dwell specially on the fact that Alexander anticipated in action what Zeno and the Stoics were soon to be teaching. This shows that the idea of a rational order is not only an attractive and a sublime conception but that

[9] Ernest Barker, Introduction to his translation of *Aristotle's Politics* (1946), p. lix.

[10] *Ibid.,* lix-lx. Cf. Saint Paul on the One Church, which was "neither Greek nor Jew . . . Barbarian, Scythian, bond nor free."

it is a necessary assumption in the government of large and heterogeneous states. Alexander came to it in spite of Aristotle's teaching to the contrary. His practical experience compelled him to see that in an empire which included the Persians as well as the Greeks there had to be a common law which was valid for both. To be valid for both the Greeks and the Persians, the law had in some significant degree to have their consent. The Persians could not be commanded and coerced.

As in fact the laws were promulgated to the Persians by Alexander, who was a Greek, it was necessary to convince the Persians that Alexander's laws reflected something that was higher than the will and the intentions of the Greeks, something that was binding on both the Greeks and the Persians. That something was the faculty of distinguishing by reason the good and the bad. For this faculty was not peculiar to the Greeks but was common to both Persians and Greeks.

Alexander had discovered empirically what Zeno was to formulate theoretically—that a large plural society cannot be governed without recognizing that, transcending its plural interests, there is a rational order with a superior common law. This common law is "natural" in the sense that it can be discovered by any rational mind, that it is not the willful and arbitrary positive command of the sovereign power.[11] This is the necessary assumption, without which it is impossible for different peoples with their competing interests to live together in peace and freedom within one community.

The Roman lawyers worked out what Alexander had anticipated and what the Stoics taught. By the time of Cicero there were, says Barker, three different bodies and conceptions of law.[12] The first, called *ius civile,* was applicable only to Roman citizens. The second was a body of commercial laws, known as the *ius gentium,* that were enforced by the Roman courts in all commercial cases: "a common law of contract throughout the empire." [13]

The *ius gentium* was meant to contain what was common and universal, separated from what was peculiar and

[11] Cf. Otto von Gierke, *Natural Law and the Theory of Society,* translated with an Introduction by Ernest Barker (1934), Vol. I, pp. 224-225.

[12] *Ibid.,* p. xxxvi.

[13] F. de Zulueta, "The Science of Law," in *The Legacy of Rome,* edited by Cyril Bailey (Oxford, Clarendon Press, 1928), p. 202.

local, in the laws of all states. And beyond this practical common law for commercial intercourse, the Roman jurists recognized that in theory there was also natural law, the *ius naturale,* which is "the law imposed on mankind by common human nature, that is, by reason in response to human needs and instincts." [14] This is not, says Barker, "a body of actual law, which can be enforced in actual courts" . . . but "a way of looking at things—a spirit of 'humane interpretation' in the mind of the judge and the jurist—which may, and does, affect the law which is actually enforced, but does so without being actual law itself."

The idea of a universal rational order became substantial and effective in the Roman law. This was the law of a great society which did in fact bring peace and order to the Western world. The remembrance of the Roman peace is stamped indelibly on the consciousness of Western men. After the fall of the Roman Empire, the Roman law, which was practiced in some degree almost everywhere, and was taught everywhere, was recognized as "the law of an international civilization and relatively universal." [15]

With the beginning of the new age, after 1500, Roman law, as codified and digested in the *Corpus Juris* of Justinian, was regarded as the concrete expression of universal human reason. When the question came to be asked, says Barker, "What does this conception of Natural Law actually contain or include?" the answer tends to be, during the Middles Ages generally and down to the rise of a new school of Natural Law after 1500, "It contains or includes the *whole* of Roman law, which is, *as a whole,* both supremely reasonable and universally diffused, and is therefore natural." [16]

5. *The Rupture in Modern Times*

THE NEW school of natural law, which flourished from about 1500 to 1800, was a response to the pluralism of the modern age; to the rise of national states, to the schism of the Church, to the explorations and to the expansion of world commerce, to the advance of science and of

[14] *Ibid.,* p. 204.
[15] *Ibid.,* p. 181.
[16] Gierke, *op. cit.,* p. xxxix.

secularism, to the progressive division and specialization of labor. As the diversity of belief, opinion and interest became greater, the need for a common criterion and for common laws became more acute.

The new school of natural law was able to meet this need until the end of the eighteenth century. That was long enough to preside over the founding of the British and the American constitutional orders, and of those which derive from them. But the school of natural law has not been able to cope with the pluralism of the later modern age—with the pluralism which has resulted from the industrial revolution and from the enfranchisement and the emancipation of the masses of the people.

In the simple and relatively homogeneous society of the eighteenth century natural law provided the principles of a free state. But then the mode of such thinking went out of fashion. In the nineteenth century little was done to remint the old ideas. They were regarded as obsolete and false, as hostile to the rise of democracy, and they were abandoned to the reactionaries. The great frame of reference to the rational order was missing. No body of specific principles and precepts was worked out in order to regulate international relations, nor to cope with the problems raised by the industrial revolution and the advance of science and technology.

Yet, in this pluralized and fragmenting society a public philosophy with common and binding principles was more necessary than it had ever been. The proof of the need is in the impulse to escape from freedom, which Erich Fromm has described so well.[17] It has been growing stronger as the emancipation of the masses of the people from authority has brought the dissolution of public, general, objective criteria of the true and the false, the right and the wrong. "I can assure you," wrote André Gide in 1928, "that the feeling of *freedom* can plunge the soul into a sort of anguish."[18]

"We know it from within, by a sort of immediate and personal experience," says Gilson, who was writing between the wars, that "Western culture was steadily following its process of dissolution."[19] Similarly, Spengler's

[17] Erich Fromm, *Escape from Freedom.*

[18] *The Journals of André Gide,* translated by Justin O'Brien (1947-51), Vol. III, 1928-1939, entry for Nov. 15, 1928, p. 26.

[19] Etienne Gilson, *The Unity of Philosophical Experience* (1937), p. 271.

famous book on *The Decline of the West* was first published in 1918 but it was written before the outbreak of the war.

But until the historic disasters of our own time, the loneliness and anxiety of modern men had been private, without public and overt political effect. As long as the public order still provided external security, their inner insecurity was still a personal and private and inward affair. Since the breakdown of public order during the First World War, there has been no security for multitudes and no ease of mind for anyone.

Observing the public disorder in which he himself had always lived, and knowing how the inner disorder provoked the impulse to escape from it, Hitler conceived his doctrine. He had the insight of genius into human weakness, and he wrote in *Mein Kampf* that the masses are "like a woman . . . who will submit to the strong man rather than dominate the weakling . . . the masses love the ruler rather than the suppliant, and inwardly they are far more satisfied by a doctrine which tolerates no rival than by the grant of liberal freedom; they often feel at a loss what to do with it, and even easily feel themselves deserted." [20]

The masses that Hitler was planning to dominate are the modern men who find in freedom from the constraints of the ancestral order an intolerable loss of guidance and of support. With Gide they are finding that the burden of freedom is too great an anxiety. The older structures of society are dissolving and they must make their way through a time of troubles. They have been taught to expect a steady progress towards a higher standard of life, and they have not been prepared to withstand the frustrations of a prolonged crisis in the outer world and the loneliness of their self-centered isolation.

They are the men who rise up against freedom, unable to cope with its insoluble difficulties and unable to endure the denial of communion in public and common truths. They have found no answer to their need and no remedy for their anguish in the principles and practice of freedom as they have known them in the liberal democracies of this century. There is a profound disorientation in their experience, a radical disconnection between the notions of their minds and the needs of their souls. They

[20] Adolf Hitler, *Mein Kampf* (1939), p. 56.

have become the "lonely crowd" [21] that Riesman has described. They are Durkheim's anomic mass.[22] They are Toynbee's proletarans who are "of" but not "in" the community they live in; for they have "no 'stake' in that community beyond the fact of its physical existence." Their "true hallmark . . . is neither poverty nor humble birth but is the consciousness—and the resentment that this consciousness inspires—of being disinherited." [23] They are, as Karl Jaspers says, men dissolved into "an anonymous mass" because they are "without an authentic world, without provenance or roots," [24] without, that is to say, belief and faith that they can live by.

[21] David Riesman, *The Lonely Crowd.*
[22] Emile Durkheim, *Suicide.*
[23] Arnold Toynbee, *A Study of History,* (1951), Vol. I, p. 41; Vol. V, p. 63.
[24] Karl Jaspers, *The Origin and Goal of History,* translated from the German edition of 1949 by Michael Bullock (London, Routledge and Kegan Paul, Ltd., 1953), pp. 127-128.

CHAPTER NINE

The Renewal of the Public Philosophy

1. *The Capacity to Believe*

THE FREEDOM which modern men are turned away from, not seldom with relief and often with enthusiasm, is the hollow shell of freedom. The current theory of freedom holds that what men believe may be important to them but that it has almost no public significance. The outer defenses of the free way of life stand upon the legal guarantees against the coercion of belief. But the citadel is vacant because the public philosophy is gone, and all that the defenders of freedom have to defend in common is a public neutrality and a public agnosticism.

Yet when we have demonstrated the need for the public philosophy, how do we prove that the need can be satisfied? [1] Not, we may be sure, by exhortation, however eloquent, to rise to the enormity of the present danger, still less by lamentations about the glory and the grandeur that are past. Modern men, to whom the argument is addressed, have a low capacity to believe in the invisible, the intangible, and the imponderable.

Exhortation can capture the will to believe. But of the will to believe there is no lack. The modern trouble is in a low capacity to believe in precepts which restrict and restrain private interests and desire. Conviction of the need of these restraints is difficult to restore once it has been radically impaired. Public principles can, of course, be imposed by a despotic government. But the public philosophy of a free society cannot be restored by fiat and by force. To come to grips with the unbelief which underlies the condition of anomy, we must find a way to re-establish confidence in the validity of public standards. We must renew the convictions from which our political morality springs.

[1] Cf. Leo Strauss, *Natural Right and History* (1953), p. 6.

In the prevailing popular culture all philosophies are the instruments of some man's purpose, all truths are self-centered and self-regarding, and all principles are the rationalizations of some special interest. There is no public criterion of the true and the false, of the right and the wrong, beyond that which the preponderant mass of voters, consumers, readers, and listeners happen at the moment to be supposed to want.

There is no reason to think that this condition of mind can be changed until it can be proved to the modern skeptic that there are certain principles which, when they have been demonstrated, only the willfully irrational can deny, that there are certain obligations binding on all men who are committed to a free society, and that only the willfully subversive can reject them.

When I say that the condition of anomy cannot be corrected unless these things are proved to the modern skeptic, I mean that the skeptic must find the proof compelling. His skepticism cannot be cured by forcing him to conform. If he has no strong beliefs, he will usually conform if he is made to conform. But the very fact that he has been forced by the government or by the crowd will prove that the official doctrine lacked something in the way of evidence or of reason to carry full conviction. In the blood of the martyrs to intolerance are the seeds of unbelief.

In order to repair the capacity to believe in the public philosophy, it will be necessary to demonstrate the practical relevance and the productivity of the public philosophy. It is almost impossible to deny its high and broad generalities. The difficulty is to see how they are to be applied in the practical affairs of a modern state.

We are back, in a manner of speaking, before the Roman lawyers worked out the *ius gentium* and related it to the *ius naturale,* back with Alexander the Great, who understood the pressing need for common laws in a plural society, and with Zeno who formulated the higher generalities. Given the practical need which is acute, and the higher generalities, which are self-evident, can we develop a positive working doctrine of the good society under modern conditions? The answer which I am making to this question is that it can be done if the ideas of the public philosophy are recovered and are re-established in the minds of men of light and leading.

2. For Example: The Theory of Property

LET US, then, put the matter to the test by applying the public philosophy to some of the great topics of our public life.

I shall begin with the theory of private property—before and after the loss of the public philosophy and the rupture of the traditions. We can do this conveniently by examining what Blackstone, working in the middle of the eighteenth century, does with the theory of private property. Blackstone's mind was formed in the classical tradition. But Blackstone's world was in movement, and he was not equal to the creative effort of using the tradition to cope with the new circumstances.

He had declared that security of the person was the first, that liberty of the individual was the second, and that property was "the third absolute right inherent in every Englishman." [2] But, as a civilized man, he had to do more than to assert the absolute right. He had "to examine more deeply the rudiments and grounds" [3] on which it could be justified rationally.

Between the lines of his elegant and stately prose one can see, I think, that Blackstone was puzzled. According to his tradition, the rational justification of property is as a system of corresponding and reciprocal rights and duties. In the public philosophy an absolute right to property, or to anything else that affects other men, cannot be entertained. To claim it is to be outside the law and the bounds of civility. This conception of property is most easily intelligible in a society where the principal forms of private property are in agricultural land. The land is visible and its products are known to all. This lends itself to a definition of the corresponding rights and duties: of the landlord with his tenants and hired workers below him in the hierarchy and above him with the sovereign power, claiming taxes and services.

When the main forms of property are intangible the difficulty of defining rights and duties is much greater. When Blackstone was writing, England was a rising com-

[2] Sir William Blackstone, *Commentaries on the Laws of England*, Book I, Ch. 1.
[3] *Ibid.*, II, 1.

mercial power and the comparatively simple problems of a society based on landed property were already overtaken by the problems of an economy in which property was owned as money, as commercial paper, as stocks and bonds. It was easy enough to assert rights to intangible property, but difficult to define the duties of intangible property. Yet unless that was done, property would not be under general laws.

Blackstone is in a way a tragic figure in that, thanks to his education, he had the intimation that the right direction was to work toward bringing intangible property under public standards. Yet for one reason or another he did not take it. He was, however, troubled. He knew that "nothing . . . so generally . . . engages the affections of mankind" as that "sole and despotic dominion which one man claims and exercises over the external things of the world, in total exclusion of the right of any other individual in the universe." But as a man steeped in the civilized traditions of the West, he knew too that there must be rational limits put upon the acquisitive and possessive instincts. As a man of the world, that is to say of his world and of the world that was to come, he knew also how little the rising men of property wished to hear about obligations that would limit their absolute rights.

So, with a certain regret, and perhaps with an intuitive foreboding, he wrote that "Pleased as we are with the possession, we seem afraid to look back to the means by which it was acquired, as if fearful of some defect in our title . . . not caring to reflect that (accurately and strictly speaking) there is no foundation in nature or in natural law, why a set of words upon parchment should convey the dominion of land: why the son should have a right to exclude his fellow-creatures from a determinate spot of ground, because his father had done so before him: or why the occupier of a particular field or of a jewel, when lying on his death-bed, and no longer able to maintain possession, should be entitled to tell the rest of the world which of them should enjoy it after him." [4]

Blackstone thought that these questions which challenge "the sole and despotic dominion" of the property holder, "would be useless and even troublesome in common life." As a man of his world he felt bound to say that "it is well if the mass of mankind will obey the laws when

[4] *Ibid.*, II, 1.

made, without scrutinizing too nicely into the reason for making them." But as one formed in the traditions of civility, he could not ignore the question of whether there was "some defect in our title" to absolute property. And as an exponent of "rational science" he felt bound to expound the classical conception of private property. He puts it this way: a man's property

> . . . consists in the free use, enjoyment and disposal of all his acquisitions, without any control or diminution, *save only by the laws of the land.* The original of private property is probably founded in nature . . . but certainly the *modifications* under which we at present find it, the method of conserving it in the present owner, and of translating it from man to man, *are entirely derived from society;* and are some of those civil advantages in exchange for which every individual has resigned a part of his natural liberty.[5]

The rights of property, that is to say, are a creation of the laws of the state. And since the laws can be altered, there are no absolute rights of property. There are legal rights to use and to enjoy and to dispose of property. The laws define what are the rights to use and to enjoy and to dispose of property, which the courts will enforce.

For, says Blackstone . . .

> The earth and all things therein are the general property of all mankind, exclusive of other beings, from the immediate gift of the creator.

It is in order that, and only in order that, the earth may be enjoyed most fully that

> . . . the legislature of England has universally promoted the grand ends of civil society, the peace and security of individuals, by steadily pursuing that wise and orderly maxim of *assigning* [Italics mine] to everything capable of ownership a legal and determinate owner.[6]

Conceived in this fashion, private property can never be regarded as giving to any man an absolute title to ex-

[5] *Ibid.,* I, 1, 3. (Italics mine).
[6] *Ibid.,* II, 1.

ercise "the sole and despotic dominion" over the land and the resources of nature. The ultimate title does not lie in the owner. The title is in "mankind," in *The People* as a corporate community. The rights of the individual in that patrimony are creations of the law, and have no other validity except as they are ordained by law. The purpose of laws which establish private property is not to satisfy the acquisitive and possessive instincts of the primitive man, but to promote "the grand ends of civil society"— which comprehend "the peace and security of individuals."

Because the legal owner enjoys the use of a limited necessity belonging to all men, he cannot be the sovereign lord of his possessions. He is not entitled to exercise his absolute and therefore arbitrary will. He owes duties that correspond with his rights. His ownership is a grant made by the laws to achieve not his private purposes but the common social purpose. And, therefore, the laws of property may and should be judged, reviewed and, when necessary, amended, so as to define the specific system of rights and duties that will promote the ends of society.

This is a doctrine of private property which denies the pretension to a "sole and despotic dominion." When Blackstone, though his conscience was troubled, accepted the sole and despotic dominion, he broke with the public philosophy and the traditions of civility. After his break the recognized theorists developed regressively the conception of private property as an absolute right. For a time they excluded from political philosophy, from jurisprudence and from legislation, almost any notion that property had duties as well as rights.

Absolute private property inevitably produced intolerable evils. Absolute owners did grave damage to their neighbors and to their descendants: they ruined the fertility of the land, they exploited destructively the minerals under the surface, they burned and cut forests, they destroyed the wild life, they polluted streams, they cornered supplies and formed monopolies, they held land and resources out of use, they exploited the feeble bargaining power of wage earners.

For such abuses of absolute property the political scientists and the law makers had no remedy. They had lost the tradition that property is the creation of the law for social purposes. They had no principles by which the law could deal with the abuses of property. The individualists of the nineteenth century could not, therefore, defend and preserve the system of private property by reforming it, and by adapting it to the circumstances of the modern age. They knew much about the rights of property and little about any corresponding duties. And so, because there was no legal remedy for the abuses of private property, because the duties which are the rational justification of property were no longer defined and enforced, the idea of private property lost its rational justification.

Between the property holders and the propertyless, who became the majority in many countries, there was, in consequence, no connecting bond, no consensus within the same realm of rational discourse. The proletariat had the duty to respect the rights of owners. But the owners owed no reciprocal duty to the proletariat. There were no obligations in which the proletarians found *their* rights. Thus there arose the ominous phenomenon of "the two nations," the confrontation of those who owned the earth by those who had nothing to lose. The latter were more numerous than the former. As they acquired votes, the main issue in the domestic politics of the democracies became the struggle between the minority who had so much absolute property and the great mass of the electorate who had so little property.

To this conflict there have been and are two possible outcomes: a gradual, cumulative, and perhaps at last a violent expropriation of the men of property—or reforms of the laws of property which restore adequate duties. But for several generations after Blackstone, the very idea of property as a system of duties was obscured. The public philosophy was discarded, and the most humane and enlightened men of the nineteenth century had little notion how rational reforms could be made. The alternatives, it appeared, were to defend absolute property against the growing discontent of the propertyless, or to abolish private property. It was a dangerous and a false dilemma. But in the nineteenth century this became the dilemma. The choice, it was said, was between individualism and collectivism, between Manchester and Marx, between absolute property maintained by the force of the few and absolute property abolished by the dictatorship of the mass.

The case of Blackstone has shown that a different and better theory of property was possible. It was possible *if* he and his successors had adhered to the public philosophy—if they had used, instead of abandoning, the principles which he stated so well. The earth is the general property of all mankind. Private titles of ownership are assigned by law-making authorities to promote the grand ends of civil society. Private property is, therefore, a system of legal rights and duties. Under changing conditions the system must be kept in accord with the grand ends of civil society.

Blackstone and his successors did not work out legal propositions from these principles.[7] As I am contending that it would have been better if they had done so, I now ask myself what is the validity of these principles? Are they devices, like the rules of the road, for regulating the traffic? If they are only that, then another set of assumptions could be just as valid, like the rule of the road in Britain that one must drive to the left. One could, and in fact men have, constructed systems of property on quite different assumptions—on the assumption, for example, that the earth is the general property of white men only, or of a master race of white men, or of those castes which have not sinned in a previous incarnation. But if the principles are more than that, if they have a validity which overrides such special claims, what is the virtue which gives them their validity?

They are the laws of a rational order of human society —in the sense that all men, when they are sincerely and lucidly rational, will regard them as self-evident. The rational order consists of the terms which must be met in order to fulfill men's capacity for the good life in this world. They are the terms of the widest consensus of rational men in a plural society. They are the propositions to which all men concerned, if they are sincerely and lucidly rational, can be expected to converge. There could never be a consensus that Africa belongs to the descendants of the Dutch settlers; a property system founded on that pretension cannot be generally acceptable, and will generate disorder. The classical doctrine has a superior validity in that a system of property based upon it may obtain a consensus of support in the community, and would have the prospect of being workable.

When we speak of these principles as natural laws, we must be careful. They are not scientific "laws" like the laws of the motions of the heavenly bodies. They do not describe human behavior as it is. They prescribe what it

[7] Cf. my *The Good Society*, Ch. 12.

should be. They do not enable us to predict what men will actually do. They are the principles of right behavior in the good society, governed by the Western traditions of civility.

It is possible to organize a state and to conduct a government on quite different principles. But the outcome will not be freedom and the good life.

3. For Example: Freedom of Speech

ONLY within a community which adheres to the public philosophy is there sure and sufficient ground for the freedom to think and to ask questions, to speak and to publish. Nobody can justify in principle, much less in practice, a claim that there exists an unrestricted right of anyone to utter anything he likes at any time he chooses. There can, for example, be no right, as Mr. Justice Holmes said, to cry "Fire" in a crowded theater. Nor is there a right to tell a customer that the glass beads are diamonds, or a voter that the opposition candidate for President is a Soviet agent.

Freedom of speech has become a central concern of the Western society because of the discovery among the Greeks that dialectic, as demonstrated in the Socratic dialogues, is a principal method of attaining truth, and particularly a method of attaining moral and political truth. "The ability to raise searching difficulties on both sides of a subject will," said Aristotle, "make us detect more easily the truth and error about the several points that arise."[8] The right to speak freely is one of the necessary means to the attainment of the truth. That, and not the subjective pleasure of utterance, is why freedom is a necessity in the good society.

This was the ground on which Milton in the *Areopagitica* opposed the order of Parliament (1643) that no book should be printed or put on sale unless it had first been licensed by the authorities:

As therefore the state of man now is; what wisdom can there be to choose, what continence to forbear without the knowledge of evil? . . . Since therefore the knowl-

[8] *Topics,* Bk. I Ch. 1, 101a35.

edge and survey of vice is in this world so necessary to the constituting of human virtue, and the scanning of error to the confirmation of truth, how can we more safely, and with less danger, scout into the regions of sin and falsity than by reading all manner of tractates and hearing all manner of reason? [9]

The method of dialectics is to confront ideas with opposing ideas in order that the pro and the con of the dispute will lead to true ideas. But the dispute must not be treated as a trial of strength. It must be a means of elucidation. In a Socratic dialogue the disputants are arguing co-operatively in order to acquire more wisdom than either of them had when he began. In a sophistical argument the sophist is out to win a case, using rhetoric and not dialectic. "Both alike," says Aristotle, "are concerned with such things as come, more or less, within the general ken of all men and belong to no definite science."[10] But while "dialectic is a process of criticism wherein lies the path to the principle of all inquiries,"[11] "rhetoric is concerned with the modes of persuasion."[12]

Divorced from its original purpose and justification, as a process of criticism, freedom to think and speak are not self-evident necessities. It is only from the hope and the intention of discovering truth that freedom acquires such high public significance. The right of self-expression is, as such, a private amenity rather than a public necessity. The right to utter words, whether or not they have meaning, and regardless of their truth, could not be a vital interest of a great state but for the presumption that they are the chaff which goes with the utterance of true and significant words.

But when the chaff of silliness, baseness, and deception is so voluminous that it submerges the kernels of truth, freedom of speech may produce such frivolity, or such mischief, that it cannot be preserved against the demand for a restoration of order or of decency. If there is a dividing line between liberty and license, it is where freedom of speech is no longer respected as a procedure of the truth and becomes the unrestricted right to exploit the

---

[9] Milton's *Areopagitica* (Oxford University Press, 1949), pp. 18-19.

[10] *Rhetoric*, Bk. I, Ch. 1, 1354a1-3.

[11] *Topics*, Bk. I, Ch. 2, 101b3-4.

[12] *Rhetoric*, Bk. I, Ch. 1, 1355a4.

ignorance, and to incite the passions, of the people. Then freedom is such a hullabaloo of sophistry, propaganda, special pleading, lobbying, and salesmanship that it is difficult to remember why freedom of speech is worth the pain and trouble of defending it.

What has been lost in the tumult is the meaning of the obligation which is involved in the right to speak freely. It is the obligation to subject the utterance to criticism and debate. Because the dialectical debate is a procedure for attaining moral and political truth, the right to speak is protected by a willingness to debate.

In the public philosophy, freedom of speech is conceived as the means to a confrontation of opinion—as in a Socratic dialogue, in a schoolmen's disputation, in the critiques of scientists and savants, in a court of law, in a representative assembly, in an open forum.

> Even at the canonisation of a saint, [says John Stuart Mill] the church admits and listens patiently to a "devil's advocate." The holiest of men, it appears, cannot be admitted to posthumous honors, until all that the devil could say against him is known and weighed. If even the Newtonian philosophy were not permitted to be questioned, mankind could not feel as complete assurance of its truth as they now [1859] do. The beliefs which we have most warrant for, have no safeguard to rest on, but a standing invitation to the whole world to prove them unfounded. If the challenge is not accepted, or is accepted and the attempts fails, we are far enough from certainty still; but we have done the best that the existing state of human reason admits of; we have neglected nothing that could give the truth the chance of reaching us: if the lists are kept open, we may hope that if there be a better truth, it will be found when the human mind is capable of receiving it; and in the meantime we may rely on having attained such approach to truth, as is possible in our day. This is the amount of certainty attainable by a fallible being, and this is the sole way of attaining it.[13]

And because the purpose of the confrontation is to dis-

[13] J. S. Mill, *On Liberty*. In *On Liberty, Representative Government, The Subjection of Women* (London, Oxford University Press, 1946), Ch. II, pp. 28-29.

cern truth, there are rules of evidence and of parliamentary procedure, there are codes of fair dealing and fair comment, by which a loyal man will consider himself bound when he exercises the right to publish opinions. For the right to freedom of speech is no license to deceive, and willful misrepresentation is a violation of its principles. It is sophistry to pretend that in a free country a man has some sort of inalienable or constitutional right to deceive his fellow men. There is no more right to deceive than there is a right to swindle, to cheat, or to pick pockets. It may be inexpedient to arraign every public liar, as we try to arraign other swindlers. It may be a poor policy to have too many laws which encourage litigation about matters of opinion. But, in principle, there can be no immunity for lying in any of its protean forms.

In our time the application of these fundamental principles poses many unsolved practical problems. For the modern media of mass communication do not lend themselves easily to a confrontation of opinions. The dialectical process for finding truth works best when the same audience hears all the sides of the disputation. This is manifestly impossible in the moving pictures: if a film advocates a thesis, the same audience cannot be shown another film designed to answer it. Radio and television broadcasts do permit some debate. But despite the effort of the companies to let opposing views be heard equally, and to organize programs on which there are opposing speakers, the technical conditions of broadcasting do not favor genuine and productive debate. For the audience, tuning on and tuning off here and there, cannot be counted upon to hear, even in summary form, the essential evidence and the main arguments on all the significant sides of a question. Rarely, and on very few public issues, does the mass audience have the benefit of the process by which truth is sifted from error—the dialectic of debate in which there is immediate challenge, reply, cross-examination, and rebuttal. The men who regularly broadcast the news and comment upon the news cannot—like a speaker in the Senate or in the House of Commons—be challenged by one of their listeners and compelled then and there to verify their statements of fact and to re-argue their inferences from the facts.

Yet when genuine debate is lacking, freedom of speech does not work as it is meant to work. It has lost the principle which regulates it and justifies it—that is to say, dialectic conducted according to logic and the rules of evidence. If there is no effective debate, the unrestricted right to speak will unloose so many propagandists, procurers, and panderers upon the public that sooner or later in self-defense the people will turn to the censors to protect them. An unrestricted and unregulated right to speak cannot be maintained. It will be curtailed for all manner of reasons and pretexts, and to serve all kinds of good, foolish, or sinister ends.

For in the absence of debate unrestricted utterance leads to the degradation of opinion. By a kind of Gresham's law the more rational is overcome by the less rational, and the opinions that will prevail will be those which are held most ardently by those with the most passionate will. For that reason the freedom to speak can never be maintained merely by objecting to interference with the liberty of the press, of printing, of broadcasting, of the screen. It can be maintained only by promoting debate.

In the end what men will most ardently desire is to suppress those who disagree with them and, therefore, stand in the way of the realization of their desires. Thus, once confrontation in debate is no longer necessary, the toleration of all opinions leads to intolerance. Freedom of speech, separated from its essential principle, leads through a short transitional chaos to the destruction of freedom of speech.

It follows, I believe, that in the practice of freedom of speech, the degree of toleration that will be maintained is directly related to the effectiveness of the confrontation in debate which prevails or can be organized. In the Senate of the United States, for example, a Senator can promptly be challenged by another Senator and brought to an accounting. Here among the Senators themselves the conditions are most nearly ideal for the toleration of all opinions.[14] At the other extreme there is the secret circulation of anonymous allegations. Here there is no means of challenging the author, and without any violation of the principles of freedom, he may properly be dealt with by detectives, by policemen, and the criminal courts. Between such extremes there are many problems of toleration which depend essentially upon how effective is the confrontation in debate. Where it is inefficient, as in the standard news-

[14] For non-Senators attacked by Senators the case is different.

paper press taken as a whole, freedom is largely unrestricted by law. Where confrontation is difficult, as in broadcasting, there is also an acceptance of the principle that some legal regulation is necessary—for example, in order to insure fair play for political parties. When confrontation is impossible, as in the moving picture, or in the so-called comic books, there will be censorship.

4. *The Limits of Dissent*

THE counterrevolutionary movements have subjected the liberal democracies to severe stresses and strains: how to insure their security and survival without abandoning their liberties. They are faced with popular movements, aided and abetted by unfriendly foreign powers, and employing the machinery of democratic governments to capture it and in order to abolish it. When they are working to attain power and before they do attain it, the fascist and communist parties invoke all the guarantees of the bill of rights, all the prerogatives of popular parties, of elections, of representation of the assemblies, of tenure in the civil service. But when they attain power, they destroy the liberal democratic institutions on which, as on a broad staircase, they climbed to power.

This exploitation of free institutions is, it seems to me, compelling proof that these institutions are inseparable from the public philosophy. If the connection is forgotten, as is so generally the case in the contemporary democracies, free institutions are poorly defended by the liberal democracies. They are the easy prey of their enemies. Either the fascists seize power in order to forestall the communists, or the communists seize power to forestall the fascists.

There is no equivocation in the public philosophy about the principle of the defense of free institutions. The rule is that the right to enjoy them and the duty to maintain them are inseparable. The right to these institutions is, that is to say, for those who adhere to them.

The criterion of loyalty is an indubitable commitment to defend and preserve the order of political and civil rights. The question of whether the liberal democratic states should outlaw, or in other ways contain, counterrevolutionary movements is not one of principle but of expediency and practical prudence. There is no doubt about the principle: that the counterrevolutionary movements are enemies of the state, and must be defeated.

In applying the principle the specific question of whether this party or that individual is or is not loyal is a matter to be determined by due process. For while there can be no right to destroy the liberal democratic state, there is an inalienable right to have the question adjudicated justly in all particular cases as to whether this person or that is an enemy of the state. This right cannot be denied to those who have not been proved guilty without denying it to all who would be proved not guilty.

The limits of dissent are not too difficult to fix when we are dealing with avowedly revolutionary parties like the communists and the fascists. The borderline between sedition and radical reform is between the denial and the acceptance of the sovereign principle of the public philosophy: that we live in a rational order in which by sincere inquiry and rational debate we can distinguish the true and the false, the right and the wrong. The counterrevolutionists, who suppress freedom in order to propagate the official doctrine, reject the procedure by which in the free society official policy is determined.

Rational procedure is the ark of the covenant of the public philosophy. There is no set of election laws or constitutional guarantees which are unchangeable. What is unchangeable is the commitment to rational determination, the commitment to act in public life on the assumption which C. S. Peirce stated as follows:

> Human opinion universally tends in the long run to a definite form, which is the truth. Let any human being have enough information and exert enough thought upon any question, and the result will be that he will arrive at a certain definite conclusion, which is the same that any other mind will reach under sufficiently favorable circumstances. . . . There is, then, to every question a true answer, a final conclusion, to which the opinion of every man is constantly gravitating. He may for a time recede from it, but give him more experience and time for consideration, and he will finally approach it. The individual may not live to reach the truth; there is a residuum of error in every individual's opinions. No matter; it remains that there is a definite opinion to which the mind of man is, on the whole and in the long run, tending. On many questions the final agreement is

already reached, on all it will be reached if time enough is given. The arbitrary will or other individual peculiarities of a sufficiently large number of minds may postpone the general agreement in that opinion indefinitely; but it cannot affect what the character of that opinion shall be when it is reached. This final opinion then is independent, not indeed of thought in general, but of all that is arbitrary and individual in thought; is quite independent of how you, or I, or any number of men, think.[15]

It is not possible to reject this faith in the efficacy of reason and at the same time to believe that communities of men enjoying freedom could govern themselves successfully.

5. *The Mirror of History*

WE FIND, then, that the principle of freedom of speech, like that of private property, falls within the bounds of the public philosophy. It can be justified, applied, regulated in a plural society only by adhering to the postulate that there is a rational order of things in which it is possible, by sincere inquiry and rational debate, to distinguish the true and the false, the right and the wrong, the good which leads to the realization of human ends and the evil which leads to destruction and to the death of civility.

The free political institutions of the Western world were conceived and established by men who believed that honest reflection on the common experience of mankind would always cause men to come to the same ultimate conclusions. Within the Golden Rule of the same philosophy for elucidating their ultimate ends, they could engage with confident hope in the progressive discovery of truth. All issues could be settled by scientific investigation and by free debate if—but only if—all the investigators and the debaters adhered to the public philosophy; if, that is to say, they used the same criteria and rules of reason for

[15] Cited in Herbert W. Schneider, *A History of American Philosophy* (1946), p. 517. From a review of Fraser's *Works of George Berkeley* in *North American Review*, Vol. CXIII (1871), pp. 455-456.

arriving at the truth and for distinguishing good and evil.

Quite evidently, there is no clear sharp line which can be drawn in any community or among communities between those who adhere and those who do not adhere to the public philosophy. But while there are many shades and degrees in the spectrum, the two ends are well-defined. When the adherence of the whole body of people to the public philosophy is firm, a true community exists; where there is division and dissent over the main principles the result is a condition of latent war.

In the maintenance and formation of a true community the articulate philosophy is, one might say, like the thread which holds the pieces of the fabric together. Not everyone can have mastered the philosophy; most people, presumably, may have heard almost nothing about it. But if among the people of light and leading the public philosophy has, as the Chinese say, the Mandate of Heaven, the beliefs and the habits which cause men to collaborate will remain whole. But if the public philosophy is discarded among them, being treated as reactionary or as nonsensical, then the stitches will have been pulled out and the fabric will come apart.

The fabrics in the metaphor are the traditions of how the good life is lived and the good society is governed. When they come apart, as they have in the Western democracies, the result is tantamount to a kind of collective amnesia. The liberal democracies have been making mistakes in peace and in war which they would never have made were they not suffering from what is a failure of memory. They have forgotten too much of what their predecessors had learned before them. The newly enfranchised democracies are like men who have kept their appetites but have forgotten how to grow food. They have the perennial human needs for law and order, for freedom and justice, for what only good government can give them. But the art of governing well has to be learned. If it is to be learned, it has to be transmitted from the old to the young, and the habits and the ideas must be maintained as a seamless web of memory among the bearers of the tradition, generation after generation.

When the continuity of the traditions of civility is ruptured, the community is threatened: unless the rupture is repaired, the community will break down into factional, class, racial and regional wars. For when the continuity is interrupted, the cultural heritage is not being transmitted. The new generation is faced with the task of re-discovering and re-inventing and relearning, by trial and error, most of what the guardians of a society need to know.

No one generation can do this. For no one generation of men are capable of creating for themselves the arts and sciences of a high civilization. Men can know more than their ancestors did if they start with a knowledge of what their ancestors had already learned. They can do advanced experiments if they do not have to learn all over again how to do the elementary ones. That is why a society can be progressive only if it conserves its traditions. The generations are, as Bernard of Chartres said, "like dwarfs seated on the shoulders of giants," enabled, therefore, to "see more things than the Ancients and things more distant."[16]

But traditions are more than the culture of the arts and sciences. They are the public world to which our private worlds are joined. This continuum of public and private memories transcends all persons in their immediate and natural lives and it ties them all together. In it there is performed the mystery by which individuals are adopted and initiated into membership in the community.

The body which carries this mystery is the history of the community, and its central theme is the great deeds and the high purposes of the great predecessors. From them the new men descend and prove themselves by becoming participants in the unfinished story.

"Where I belong," says Jaspers, "and what I am living for, I first learned in the mirror of history."[17] When the individual becomes civilized he acquires a second nature. This second nature is made in the image of what he is and is living for and should become. He has seen the image in the mirror of history. This second nature, which rules over the natural man, is at home in the good society. This second nature is no proletarian but feels itself to be a rightful proprietor and ruler of the community. Full allegiance to the community can be given only by a man's second nature, ruling over his first and primitive nature, and treating it as not finally himself. Then the disciplines and the necessities and the constraints of a civilized life

[16] Cited in Étienne Gilson, *The Spirit of Medieval Philosophy* (1940), p. 426.
[17] Karl Jaspers, *Origin and Goal of History* (1953), p. 271.

have ceased to be alien to him, and imposed from without. They have become his own inner imperatives.[18]

6. Man's Second Nature

IN THE dialogues recounting the death of Socrates, Plato has painted the classic portrait of the civilized citizen. On the afternoon of his execution, Socrates is arguing with his friends. The jailers have left the door of the prison open, and Socrates is explaining why he refuses to escape.

> . . . The Athenians have thought fit to condemn me, and accordingly I have thought it better and more right to remain here and undergo my sentence; for I am inclined to think that these muscles and bones of mine would have gone off long ago to Megara or Boeotia—by the dog of Egypt they would, if they had been moved only by their own idea of what was best, and if I had not chosen as the better and nobler part, instead of playing truant and running away, to undergo any punishment which the state inflicts. There is surely a strange confusion of causes and conditions in all this. It may be said, indeed, that without bones and muscles and other parts of the body I cannot execute my purposes. But to say that I do as I do because of them, and that this is the way in which mind acts, and not from the choice of the best, is a very careless and idle mode of speaking.[19]

Socrates is saying that he, himself, is not the organism of his muscles and his bones, his reflexes, affections and instincts. He, Socrates, is the person who governs that organism. He exercises what Saint Thomas Aquinas called "a royal and politic rule" over his "irascible and concupiscible powers." These powers of the organism, its first nature, are, as Cardinal Newman said, "ever insurgent against reason." But Socrates is the ruler of that organism. He is the "I" who can "if *I* had not chosen" to rule *them,* then *they* would have rebelled and run away. This Socrates who rules *them* is the adopted and initiated

---

[18] Cf. my *Preface to Morals.*
[19] *Phaedo,* 98-99. In *The Dialogues of Plato,* translated by B. Jowett (1937).

citizen of Athens. *They* are the appetites and instincts of the natural man. For one who is ruled by his appetites is a barbarian, and quite incapable of being an Athenian citizen.

The friends of Socrates, who were there on that last day, would perhaps have said that it was only "human" that he should want to run away when he had the chance. But Socrates chose to affirm the opposite, to insist that he was most fully human because he was willing and able to govern his desires.

Needless to say the lesson of this great story is not servility and conformism, and it does not carry any implication that the people of Athens who condemned Socrates were right in their judgment. As Crito says, when he has closed his eyes, "of all the men of his time whom I have known he was the wisest and justest and best." The point of the story is that Socrates would not save himself because an Athenian citizen could not cheat the law, least of all for his own personal advantage.[20] If Athens was to be governed, it must be by citizens who by their second natures preferred the laws to the satisfaction of their own impulses, even to their own will to live. Unless the citizens would govern themselves with such authority, the Athenian city would be ungovernable. If they followed their first natures, Athens would be trampled down in the stampede.

This is the image of a man who has become fit to rule. He is ruled within by his second and civilized nature. His true self exercises the power of life and death over his natural self. For it is the true person who has qualified as proprietor of the laws and institutions of Athens and of the ideal of life which they serve. The necessities and the purposes of Athenian life are not something outside of Socrates, something alien, extraneous, imposed and only reluctantly conformed with. They are the ends of his own true character, established in that part of his being which he calls himself.

This is the inwardness of the ruling man—whatever his titles and his rank—that for the sake of his realm, of his order, of his regiment, of his ship, of his cause, he is the noble master of his own weaker and meaner passions. Although this is the aristocratic code, it is not inherent in prerogative and birth. It is functional to the capacity to rule. It is because aristocrats have been rulers, and not be-

20 *Ibid.*, 118.

cause they were born into the aristocracy, that they have held themselves to the aristocratic virtues. When, like the French nobles on the eve of the Revolution, they have lost the self-mastery which is the principle of the ruling man, they are unable to rule. Then, if they cling too long to their privileges, many of them will lose their noble heads.

CHAPTER TEN

The Two Realms

1. *The Confusion of the Realms*

AGAINST man living in the civilized tradition, who like Socrates rules his private impulses by the laws of the public world, there are arrayed the great adversaries. They tempt him with a total promise—that in a short and glorious struggle they will take him into the earthly heaven where he will realize all his hopes. The root of the matter is in these two conceptions of the human condition, and the ultimate issue is in the conflict between them.

As the bitter end has become visible in the countries of the total revolution, we can see how desperate is the predicament of modern men. The terrible events show that the harder they try to make earth into heaven, the more they make it a hell.

Yet, the yearning for salvation and for perfection is most surely not evil, and it is, moreover, perennial in the human soul. Are men then doomed by the very nature of things to be denied the highest good if it cannot be materialized in this world and if, as so large a number of modern men assume, it will not be materialized in another world?

The answer to this question is known. It can be had by recognizing the difference between the realm of existence where objects are materialized to our senses, and the realm of essence, where they are present to the mind. I am using the ambiguous but irreplaceable word "essence" as meaning the true and undistorted nature of things. The understanding of our relation to these two realms of being is exceedingly difficult to communicate, so difficult that, as a matter of fact, it has remained an esoteric wisdom.

Yet if there is a way out of the modern predicament, it begins, I believe, where we learn to recognize the difference between the two realms. For the radical error of the modern democratic gospel is that it promises, not the good life of this world, but the perfect life of heaven. The root of the error is the confusion of the two realms—that of this world where the human condition is to be born, to live, to work, to struggle and to die, and that of the transcendent world in which men's souls can be regenerate and at peace. The confusion of these two realms is an ultimate disorder. It inhibits the good life in this world. It falsifies the life of the spirit.

2. *The Good in This World*

THE IDEALS of the good life and of the good society fall far short of perfection, and in speaking of them we must not use superlatives. They are worldly ideals, which raise no expectations about the highest good. Quite the contrary. They are concerned with the best that is possible among mortal and finite, diverse and conflicting men. Thus the ideals of freedom, justice, representation, consent, law, are of the earth, earthy. They are for men who are still (as Saint Paul says in Timothy I, 9-10) under the law. For

> . . . the law is not made for a righteous man, but for the lawless and disobedient, for the ungodly and for sinners, for unholy and profane, for murderers of fathers and murderers of mothers, for manslayers,
>
> For whoremongers, for them that defile themselves with mankind, for menstealers, for liars, for perjured persons . . .

The word "freedom" has several meanings. But none would have occurred to anyone who had not been in the human condition of diversity and conflict, who had not known the issues of life among wordly men and the finitude of his own powers.

We can, for example, distinguish three principal meanings to the term. Each has been the formative principle of a school of thought.

There is Hobbes, who said that "liberty or freedom, signifieth (properly) the absence of opposition."[1] In his use of the word, we are free in respect to all the actions which no one else prevents us from doing.

---

[1] Thomas Hobbes, *Leviathan* (Oxford, Clarendon Press, 1943) Part II, Ch. XXI.

There is a meaning given to the word "liberty" by Locke: "the power a man has to do or forebear doing any particular action."[2] Here we are not free merely because we *may* do something; we must also be able to do it,—we must have the faculty for doing it and the means to do it.

The word "freedom" has still another meaning in the classical and Christian tradition. As Montesquieu put it, freedom "can consist only in the power of doing what we ought to will, and in not being constrained to do what we ought not to will."[3] We are free if we have the faculty of knowing what we *ought* to do and the will to do it.

These are not merely verbal differences, arising from ambiguity or equivocation. They are rather facets of a complex idea. For when any one of the meanings is put to a practical test, almost invariably we have to turn to the other meanings to correct its deficiencies. It is, therefore, impossible to choose one meaning, rejecting all the others, or, in fact, to come to rest in a conclusion which fixes a total meaning.

There is no final resting point, because "in the flux of things," as William James says, "things are off their balance. Whatever equilibrium our finite experiences attain to are but provisional . . . everything is in . . . a surrounding world of other things." And "if you leave it to work there, it will inevitably meet with friction and opposition from its neighbors. Its rivals and enemies will destroy it unless it can buy them off by compromising some part of its original pretentions."[4]

Words like liberty, equality, fraternity, justice, have various meanings which reflect the variability of the flux of things. The different meanings are rather like different clothes, each good for a season, for certain weather and for a time of day, none good for all times. In the infinite change and diversity of the actual world, our conceptual definitions are never exactly and finally the whole truth. For, as James said, while "the essence of life is its continually changing character . . . our concepts are all discontinuous and fixed." Like a winter overcoat, none can

---

[2] John Locke, *An Essay Concerning Human Understanding*, edited by A. C. Fraser. (Oxford, Clarendon Press, 1894), Vol. I, Bk. II, Ch. XXI, Sec. 15.

[3] Charles de Montesquieu, *The Spirit of Laws*, Bk. XI, 3.

[4] William James, *A Pluralistic Universe*. In *Essays in Radical Empiricism and A Pluralistic Universe* (1947), pp. 88, 90.

be worn with equal comfort in January and in July. Yet the summer will end, it too being subject to change. There will come a season and a time for wearing the warmer coat. So it is a mistake to think that we could wear the same coat all the time, and a mistake to throw it away, supposing in the summer that it will never be winter again.

This is the human condition. To it, in the traditions of civility, is addressed the worldly wisdom of the good life.

In this actual world of diversity and change, how do we find the right rule? We shall not find it, says Aristotle, if we look for more "clearness" than "the subject matter admits of."[5] "Matters concerned with conduct and what is good for us have no fixity," and, he added, "the agents themselves must in each case consider what is appropriate to the occasion."[6]

But the agents, we may note, do not improvise a rule which they consider appropriate to the occasion. They "consider" something. And that something, says Aristotle, is that "it is the nature of things"—including the nature of the worldly virtues—"to be destroyed by defect and excess." The problem, then, is to discern "the mean"—the point between excess and defect where the good, which the virtue aims at, is preserved.

That would be less difficult to do than in fact it is if the mean between excess and defect were a fixed point. But it is not. The defect of courage, says Aristotle, is cowardice, as when a man "flies from and fears everything and does not stand his ground against anything." The excess of courage is the rashness of a man "who fears nothing at all but goes to meet every danger." But to say this does not fix the mean in such a way that each man knows, as he knows when the traffic light is red or green, just when he should stand his ground and when he should not.

To expect to be given—to expect not to have to judge and find—the fixed points which are the mean in each particular case is, says Aristotle, to ask for more precision than can be given to this subject. We must not think of the mean as being a fixed point between the extremes. When we do that, we are allowing ourselves to suppose that the mean is the point at which a kind of bargain is struck between 50 per cent of excess and 50 per cent of

[5] *Nicomachean Ethics,* Book I, Ch. 2, 1094b. 12.
[6] *Ibid.,* Book II, Ch. 2, 1104a. 9.

deficiency. But that is not the true mean. Courage is not half cowardice and half rashness. Temperance is not half self-indulgence and half complete abstinence. The true mean is at the tension of push and pull, of attraction and resistance among the extremes.

The outcome, as Aristotle said it would be, is imprecise and inconclusive, and there is little reason to think that the wisdom of the world can ever rise above these imperfections.

3. *The Law and the Prophets*

NOR DOES the wisdom of the spirit solve precisely the perplexing problems of worldly conduct. For it is the vision of a realm of being in which the problems of earthly existence are not solved but transcended.

In the immediate, urgent, and particular issues of daily life the major prophets, the seers and the sages, have remarkably little to offer by way of practical advice and specific guidance. The deposit of wisdom in the Bible and in the classic books does not contain a systematic and comprehensive statement of moral principles from which it is possible to deduce with clarity and certainty specific answers to concrete questions. He who goes to this wisdom looking for guidance of this sort will be disappointed. If he finds it there, he must come to it by analogy and by inference. The specific rules of conduct are not explicitly there. Were they there, the history of mankind would have been different. For terrible wars and poisonous hatreds arise among men who draw irreconcilably different practical conclusions from the same general principles.

There is a hiatus between the highest wisdom and the actual perplexities with which men must deal. An encyclopedia of all that the prophets and the philosophers have taught will not tell a man clearly and definitely how to make laws, how to govern a state, how to educate his children—how, in fact, to decide the problems that the priest encounters in the confessional, the doctor with his patients, the lawyer with his clients, the judge with the litigants, the man of affairs in his business.

Faced with practical decisions, they need to know what choice they should make among the alternatives. But concrete guidance of this sort can be found only incidentally in the words of the prophets and the philosophers. They have not compiled systematic codes of specific rules for concrete cases. These codes are in the books of the scribes, the casuists, the lawgivers and the judges, and their authority is imputed. It rests on the assumption that the specific rules of conduct are implicit in the inspired utterance, and have merely been deduced from it.

The recorded sayings of Jesus and the Apostles do not contain a comprehensive body of laws and of precepts for the ordering of men's lives. In fact the Apostles seem not to have realized the need of a clear record of the sacred deposit. According to Eusebius (VI, L-4), when Peter in Rome learned that Mark remembered his sayings and was writing them down, "he neither directly forbade nor encouraged it." The voluminous and very detailed corpus of Christian laws is the work of popes, bishops, councils, canonists, casuists, doctors and writers of textbooks.

The work began immediately after the apostolic age. The Reverend Thomas J. Slater, S.J., the author of a leading Catholic manual of moral theology for English-speaking countries, says that "the Gospels contain a short summary of the teaching of Jesus Christ; this is developed somewhat in certain directions in the other writings of the New Testament, but the preachers of the Word soon found it convenient to have by them brief summaries of the moral teaching of our Lord by itself."[7] In response to this need there was written, as early as the end of the first century, such works as the *Didache, or the Teaching of the Twelve Apostles* and the *Pastor of Hermas*. The *Didache,* says Father Slater, is the first handbook of morals which comes down to us. It lays down the two moral principles of love of God and of neighbor, and then— because it is a book addressed to the practical difficulties of men—it sets out to specify the principal positive and negative duties that men owe to their parents, children, servants, neighbors and the poor. The working out of comprehensive systems of specific rules for life in this world became necessary in connection with the penitential system which was organized in the sixth, seventh and eight centuries.[8] When the Fourth Lateran Council in 1215 made confession of sin obligatory upon the faithful at least once a year, it was necessary to have comprehen-

---

[7] Thomas J. Slater, *A Manual of Moral Theology for English-Speaking Countries* (5th ed.), Vol. II, p. 308.

[8] J. C. Ayer, *A Source Book for Ancient Church History* (1913), p. 624.

sive reference books to guide the priest in the confessional concerning the great variety of human issues.[9]

The great multitudes of men everywhere and always have demanded detailed codes of conduct. They are necessary to their comfort, their convenience and their peace of mind, and no religion with a mass following is without its manuals of casuistry, its Koran, its Talmud, its Calvin's Institutes. For those who can live by the spirit alone have always been a mere handful, little groups here and there, shut away from and exalted above the normal life of their times. Without the casuists, who legislate the specific rules, translating and transmuting the inspired words into an intelligible system of ceremonial and legal precepts, the vision of the seer could not make much contact with the existential world.

4. *The Realm of the Spirit*

FOR THE vision is not of this world but of another and radically different one. The Apostles, as a matter of fact, believed themselves to be living in the last days of the world, and they made no provision for a systematic and definitive record of the sacred deposit. But even if they had not believed that the end of the existing world was near, it would still be true that what they taught is not addressed to this world but to a very different one.

There is, for example, the precept that we should love our enemies. It has troubled the doctors of the Church as it has the common man. Aquinas remarks that the good do not bear with the wicked to the extent of enduring the injuries done to God and their neighbors; St. Chrysostom says that "it is praiseworthy to be patient under one's own wrongs, but the height of impiety to dissemble injuries done to God."[10]

The saying disintegrates when we attempt to treat it as a specific rule of political conduct. What, then, is its wisdom? It is not the wisdom of the public world and of how

[9] *Encyclopedia of Religion and Ethics,* Vol. III, p. 241. *Catholic Encyclopedia,* Vol. III, pp. 416-417. The *Summa de Poenitentia et Matrimonio* was produced in 1235. From then on, until the publication of the last edition of the *Theologia Moralis* by St. Alphonsus Maria de Liguori in 1785, there was an enormous output of specific rules.

[10] Edward A. Westermarck, *The Origin and Development of the Moral Ideas* (1912-1917), Vol. I, pp. 77-78.

to govern it. It is the wisdom of the economy of our passions, and of their education and their ordering. It does not give the rules of behavior in the actual world. It sets before men a vision of themselves transformed.

Quite evidently the ideal of non-resistance would, if literally and consistently followed, abandon the world to the predatory. Poverty, universally practiced, would sink the world in squalor and darkness. Universal celibacy would extinguish human life. All this is so obvious that, manifestly, these ideas, which we find in all high religion, cannot be treated as public rules of human conduct. They are, however, related to human conduct. For they affect the nature of man, in that the vision of ourselves transformed can modify our appetites and our passions.

They are not the practical ideals of the existential world. They are the ideals of a realm of being where men are redeemed and regenerated and the evils of the world have been outgrown. While they are on earth and belong to a human society, men cannot enter that realm. But they can be drawn toward that realm. They cannot be drawn out of the carnal world. But they can be drawn away from its excesses, and, by imitation, they can become in some measure nearer to that which they would be if they had become perfect.

A man who has humility will have acquired in the last reaches of his beliefs the saving doubt of his own certainty. Though he produces wealth and uses it, and though he resists evil, he will have little acquisitiveness and possessiveness, he will have no final attachment to things, he will have no strong lust for power or for vengeance. He cannot and he will not be perfect. But in some measure he will be pulled toward perfection.

Knowledge of the other realm is not communicable in the prosaic language of the familiar material world. For it comes from a vision of a world which is not to be perceived by our senses. The language of the seers cannot be direct statements of propositions. They must speak in poetic parable and metaphor which intimates and may evoke that which is inexpressible in prose. These parables and metaphors are addressed not to the government of men, but, in the language of Saint Paul, to the creation of the new man. Who is this new man? In the famous chapter of Galatians,[11] Paul explains that the Scripture, mean-

[11] Galatians, III: 22-24.

ing the law and the prophets of the Old Testament, "hath concluded all under sin." They are addressed to unregenerate men, to men as they are in the world, to the sons of Adam and Eve who have suffered what Aquinas called a "wounding of nature." In them, "reason" has lost "its perfect hold over the lower parts of the soul."

"The law," says Saint Paul, "was our schoolmaster." It corrected our ignorance, malice, weakness and lust. But after the faith in Christ is come, "we are no longer under a schoolmaster." When our passions are transformed by allegiance to the other realm of being, we do not need to be disciplined. The regenerate man, says Saint Paul, is not conformed to this world, but is transformed in the renewing of his mind.[12] In the City of God, says St. Augustine, "sin shall have no power to delight," and men will "not be able to sin."[13] They are led of the spirit and have been "redeemed." They can, as Confucius said, follow what their hearts desire without transgressing what is right.

5. The Balance of Powers

As a MAN awakens from his primordial condition where, as Bacon said, custom is the principal magistrate of his life, he finds himself living in two worlds and subject to two allegiances. There is the familiar world which he knows through his senses and there is a world of which he has only intimations and knows only through the eyes of his mind. He is drawn between the two disparate realms of being, and the tension within them is the inexhaustible theme of human discourse. To neither can he give his whole allegiance. Their prevailing contrasts are his wretchedness. Their occasional harmonies in the lives of saints and the deeds of heroes and the excellence of genius are his glory.

In the traditions of civility, the prevailing view has been that the two realms are inseparable but disparate, and that man must work out his destiny in the balance, which is never fixed finally between the two.

This is a view which has, however, always been challenged. There are the hedonists who would withdraw wholly *into* the realm of existence, to eat, drink, and be

[12] Romans, XII: 2.
[13] *The City of God*, XXII, 30.

merry without the pains and the qualms that go with immortal yearnings. The view of civility has been challenged by the ascetics who would withdraw *from* the realm of existence, waiting for the end of the world and their own release from mortality. It has been challenged by the primitive Chiliasts, who live in the expectation that the millennium, according to the revelation of Saint John, is near at hand. And it has been challenged by the modern perfectionists who believe that by their own revolutionary acts men can make themselves the creators of heaven on this earth. In all these views the error stems from the same fundamental disorder. All refuse to recognize that, on the one hand, the two realms cannot be fused, and that, on the other hand, they cannot be separated and isolated —that they must be related by striking, maintaining, redressing a balance between them.

This is a complex and subtle truth, rather like a surd in mathematics which cannot be expressed in the finite terms of ordinary quantities.

Because we are drawn between the two realms, there can be no definitive line of demarcation of the orbits of the state and of the church. Though the political government is concerned primarily with the affairs of the existential world, though the churches are primarily committed to the realm of the spirit, they meet whenever and wherever there are issues of right and wrong, issues of what is the nature of man, of what is his true image, his place in the scheme of things, and his destiny. Both the state and the churches are involved in these decisions, and their relationship cannot be defined by any clear, precise demarcation of their respective spheres of influence.

In the tension between them, which is the theme of so much of the history of the Western society, neither must be allowed to conquer and absorb the other. The experience of the West has taught that lesson. But it has taught, also, that the two realms cannot be separated, that they cannot be isolated and insulated in different compartments. There is little room for freedom under the absolute power of a totalitarian church which dominates the secular force of the government, and none under a totalitarian state which has absorbed the spiritual powers into the secular. The best that is possible in the human condition, and in the world as it is, is that the state and the churches should each be too strong to be conquered, not strong enough to have unlimited dominion. It is in the righting of the balance between them that reason escapes from the oppressions of excessive power, and can realize its opportunities.

But while the separation of the powers of the churches and of the state is essential to a right relationship between them, the negative rule is not the principle of their right relationship. Church and state need to be separate, autonomous, and secure. But they must also meet on all the issues of good and evil.

These issues arise concretely in the fixing of public policy about the family, marriage, divorce, the authority of the father and of the mother, the guardianship of children, education, inheritance, the distribution of wealth, crime and punishment, standards of taste, loyalty and allegiance, righteous and unrighteous war. These issues, as Pope Leo XIII said in the Encyclical *Immortale Dei* (1885), belong "to the jurisdiction and judgment of both" the ecclesiastical and the civil power. In all these matters the final word is in neither of the two realms of being. There is in truth no final word. Instead there are the provisional points of equilibrium of an unending tension among variable elements. Where exactly the point of equilibrium will be in a particular place and at a particular time cannot be defined *a priori*. It must be judged empirically within the postulates of the public philosophy. For the elements which have to come into equilibrium are variables. That is why governing is not engineering but an art. That is why the same constitution and codes of laws cannot, like the plans for a jet engine, be used by all countries at any time or by any country all the time.

6. *The Mechanics of the Balance*

THE IDEA of the balancing of powers among states and within them has been used so long by so many, in such different circumstances and with such different intentions, that it is not, as a recent critic puts it, "free from philological, semantic and theoretical confusion." [14]

[14] Ernst B. Haas, "The Balance of Power: Prescription, Concept or Propaganda?" *World Politics*, Vol. V, No. 4 (July 1953). This article is a useful inventory of definitions and applied meanings of the term "balance of power" in the field of international relations.

Yet this is not a reason for agreeing with Cobden that the idea is "an undescribed, indescribable, incomprehensible nothing."[15]

If a term has many diverging definitions, it is better to begin by assuming that it is full of meanings. For none of the main ideas of our civilization has a single meaning.[16]

But in the great ideas there is some kind of central validity around which disagreements and a variety of meanings continue to revolve. Every one of the great ideas is confusing, because it is too full of meaning to be defined simply. But if it were empty of meaning, it would have disappeared into the void along with last week's argument between two drunken men.

Anyone using a complex term like "the balance of power" must, of course, say what he means by it. I start with Hobbes, who said that "in the natural state of men when there is no government and no law, there is a war of every man against every man."[17]

Hobbes did not say that everyone is in fact trying to kill everyone else but that there is "a perpetual and restless desire of power after power, that ceaseth only in death . . . and that this competition of riches, honor, command, or other powers incline us to contention, enmity and war because the way of one competitor to the attaining of his desires is to kill, subdue, supplement, or repel the other."[18]

But how out of the anarchy of warring powers can a government arise which is strong enough to impose law and order, and how can men be induced to respect the laws? Granted that out of the struggle of the rival lords, a victor will emerge as sovereign lord who rules all the others: the question is how one lord among other lords can become strong enough to overcome all the others. The answer is that almost never can he do this by pitting his strength against that of all the others jointly; rarely, too, can he do that by pitting his strength against each of them separately, one after the other. The general rule is that he must be able to take advantage of and, in measure, to contrive a situation where his rivals oppose each other. When their forces are balanced against one an-

---

[15] Cited by Haas from Richard Cobden, *Political Writings* (London, 1878), pp. 111-114.
[16] Cf. *The Great Ideas, a Syntopicon*, Mortimer J. Adler, Editor.
[17] Hobbes, *op. cit.*, Part I, Ch. 13.
[18] *Ibid.*, Part I, Ch. 11.

other, they are neutralized, and his power may then be sufficient to govern them.

This, we may say, is the mechanical principle by which the perpetual and restless desire for power after power is brought into an order. The desire for power has to be reduced. This can rarely be done, and never for long, by an omnipotent ruler. Tyranny, as Aristotle observed long ago, is short-lived.[19] Nor can the desire for power be reduced sufficiently by education and exhortation. As Montesquieu said, ". . . constant experience shows us that every man invested with power is apt to abuse it, and to carry his authority as far as it will go. Is it not strange, though true, to say that virtue itself has needs of limits? To prevent this abuse it is necessary from the very nature of things that power should be checked by power."[20]

In the measure that power is checked by power, that opposing powers are in balance, neither can prevail. Both are constrained within a common situation. In this condition, when the ponderable forces are in balance, neither being able or willing to exert decisive force, the imponderable means of reason become efficacious.

Inter arma silent leges. In the clash of arms the laws are silent. We may add that in the truce of arms the laws are heard.

Like any technical procedure, the balancing of power to neutralize power can be used for good, bad and indifferent ends. There are many who would say that the good end which politicians always profess is merely the rationalization of the perpetual and restless desire for power after power. "The truth of the matter," said Nicholas Spykman,[21] "is that states are interested only in a balance which is in their favor . . . the balance desired is the one which neutralizes other states, leaving the home state free to be the deciding force and the deciding voice."

But of what "matter" is this the "truth"? That particular states and, we may add, particular parties, factions, and individual politicians, are interested "in a balance which is in their favor." No doubt they are. No doubt they have Hobbes' desire for power after power. This is

[19] *Politics*, Book V, Ch. 12, 1315b13.
[20] Montesquieu, *op. cit.*, Book XI, Sec. 4.
[21] N. Spykman, *American Strategy in World Politics* (1942), pp. 21-25.

the truth about the first, or fallen nature of men. But this is not a truth about the balance of power. It is the truth about the condition which the balance of power can be used to correct.

Each contender for power, we must assume, will seek to win the contest—to become the ruler, and to exercise the deciding voice. But there remains still what the ruler —*when* he has the deciding voice—is interested in deciding. Will he use the position he has achieved in the system of forces in order to aggrandize his own power, and to increase his own privileges? Or is his chief interest in the order itself—that is to say, in the nation, the commonwealth, the great community—in its survival and in its harmony and in its development?

There is a radical difference between being a contender for power, a rival among rivals, and being the guardian of the order which intends to regulate all the rivalries. In the one, the technique of the balance of power is used as an instrument of aggression and defense. In the other, it is used as the structural principle of public order in the good society.

CHAPTER ELEVEN

The Defense of Civility

1. *The Thesis Restated*

WE HAVE now made a reconnaissance in the public philosophy in order to test the chances of its revival. Our warrant for making this attempt rests on certain general findings about the condition of the Western world.

The first is that free institutions and democracy were conceived and established by men who adhered to a public philosophy. Though there have been many schools in this philosophy, there are fundamental principles common to all of them: that, in Cicero's words, "law is the bond of civil society," and that all men, governors and the governed, are always under, are never above, laws; that these laws can be developed and refined by rational discussion, and that the highest laws are those upon which all rational men of good will, when fully informed, will tend to agree.

The second finding from which we have proceeded, in our inquiry, is that the modern democracies have abandoned the main concepts, principles, precepts, and the general manner of thinking which I have been calling the public philosophy. I hold that liberal democracy is not an intelligible form of government and cannot be made to work except by men who possess the philosophy in which liberal democracy was conceived and founded. The prospects of liberal democracy in this time of mighty counterrevolutions are, therefore, bound up with the question whether the public philosophy is obsolete or whether it can be revived, reunited and renewed.

I believe that the public philosophy can be revived, and the reconnaissance which we have made has been a demonstration that when it is applied to such central concepts as popular sovereignty, property, freedom of speech, and education, the public philosophy clarifies the problems and opens the way towards rational and acceptable solutions. The revival of the public philosophy depends on whether its principles and precepts—which were articulated before the industrial revolution, before the era of rapid technological change, and before the rise of the mass democracies—depends on whether this old philosophy can be reworked for the modern age. If this cannot be done, then the free and democratic nations face the totalitarian challenge without a public philosophy which free men believe in and cherish, with no public faith beyond a mere official agnosticism, neutrality and indifference. There is not much doubt how the struggle is likely to end if it lies between those who, believing, care very much—and those who, lacking belief, cannot care very much.

2. The Communication of the Public Philosophy

WE COME now to the problem of communicating the public philosophy to the modern democracies. The problem has been, to be sure, only too obvious from the beginning. For, as we have seen, the public philosophy is in a deep contradiction with the Jacobin ideology, which is, in fact, the popular doctrine of the mass democracies. The public philosophy is addressed to the government of our appetites and passions by the reasons of a second, civilized, and, therefore, acquired nature. Therefore, the public philosophy cannot be popular. For it aims to resist and to regulate those very desires and opinions which are most popular. The warrant of the public philosophy is that while the regime it imposes is hard, the results of rational and disciplined government will be good. And so, while the right but hard decisions are not likely to be popular when they are taken, the wrong and soft decisions will, if they are frequent and big enough, bring on a disorder in which freedom and democracy are destroyed.

If we ask whether the public philosophy can be communicated to the democracies, the answer must begin with the acknowledgment that there must be a doctrine to communicate. The philosophy must first be made clear and pertinent to our modern anxieties. Our reconnaissance has been addressed to that first need.

But beyond it lies the problem of the capacity and the willingness of modern men to receive this kind of philosophy. The concepts and the principles of the public philosophy have their being in the realm of immaterial entities. They cannot be experienced by our sense organs or even, strictly speaking, imagined in visual or tangible terms. Yet these essences, these abstractions, which are out of sight and out of touch, are to have and to hold men's highest loyalties.

The problem of communication is posed because in the modern world, as it is today, most men—not all men, to be sure, but most active and influential men—are in practice positivists who hold that the only world which has reality is the physical world. Only seeing is believing. Nothing is real enough to be taken seriously, nothing can be a matter of deep concern, which cannot, or at least might not, somewhere and sometime, be seen, heard, tasted, smelled, or touched.

Julius Caesar was a real person because we feel sure we could have seen him in Rome had we been there in his lifetime. By the same kind of popular common sense, communities have believed that werewolves were real. Had not a woman named Thiebenne Paget admitted that she was one of the wolves that was seen on July 18, 1603, in the District of Couvres?[1] To common sense the real is what, but only what, we believe has weight, mass, energy.

> . . . What's Hecuba to him, or he to Hecuba, that he
> should weep for her?

What are the ideas and ideals, the laws and the obligations, of the rational order if, like Hecuba, they are not flesh and blood?

Common sense is positivist and credulous, and the usual human way of satisfying it has been to materialize ideas when those ideas had to be treated as real. Men have incarnated the gods, they have re-embodied their ancestors, they have personified the laws, they have hypostasized their ideas. They have made the abstractions and universals intelligible in concrete terms, and so matters of genuine concern, by connecting them with the realties of everyday experience.

The difficulty of communicating imponderable truths to common sense is not a new one. Through the ages truths that could not be materialized have been regarded as esoteric, and communicable only to an initiated few.

[1] *The World's Great Folktales,* arranged and edited by James R. Foster (1953), p. 135.

The Gospels state that there were mysteries which Jesus could unveil only to a few. He said, "He who has ears to hear, let him hear."[2] But—

> "When he was alone, those who were about him with the twelve asked him concerning the parables. And he said to them, "To you has been given the secret of the kingdom of God, but for those outside everything is in parables . . ." [3]

Only privately to his own disciples, says Mark, did he explain "everything"; to "the whole crowd" he spoke the word "as they were able to hear it; he did not speak to them without a parable."

Why? Because, says Dante, the divine mysteries are beyond the reach of human understanding—

> It is needful to speak thus to your wit, since only through objects of sense does it apprehend that which it afterwards would make worthy of the intellect. For this the scripture condescends to your capacity, and attributes feet and hands to God, and means otherwise.[4]

There is a need to condescend to our capacity because, as Paul Tillich puts it, "It is impossible to be concerned about something which cannot be encountered concretely, be it in the realm of reality or in the realm of imagination . . . the more concrete a thing is, the more the possible concern about it. The completely concrete being, the individual person, is the object of the most radical concern —the concern of love." There is in consequence, he says, an "inescapable inner tension in the idea of God" —between God conceived as transcending all that is particular and finite, on the one hand, and the concreteness of an image of God on the other. In order to have a human concern there is needed a "being to being relationship . . . a concrete God, a God with whom man can deal" in his religious experience.[5]

While Tillich is a theologian examining the meaning

---

[2] The Gospel According to St. Mark, IV:9.

[3] Ibid., IV: 10-12.

[4] Divine Comedy, translated by C. E. Norton (1941), Paradise, Canto IV, verses 40-45.

[5] Paul Tillich, Systematic Theology (1951), Vol. I, Part II, p. 211.

of God, which he defines as the "name for that which concerns men ultimately," his findings illuminate the problem which we are studying. How can men be concerned effectively with ideas and ideals that transcend their personal experience and cannot be verified empirically in the realm of existence? The principles of the good society call for a concern with an order of being—which cannot be proved existentially to the sense organs—where it matters supremely that the human person is inviolable, that reason shall regulate the will, that truth shall prevail over error.

Because it is difficut to care about that which is not concrete, there is, in Tillich's language, "a tension in human experience." In order to become concerned about, to feel committed to, transcendent objects, we have to believe in them: to believe in them they must be concrete, they must in fact or in imagination be drawn into the orbit of our sense organs. But as we condescend in this fashion to our capacity, attributing foot and hand to God, the belief becomes involved with, often dependent upon, the materialization. Because of this dependence, the belief is vulnerable. For a little knowledge, as for example that the foot and hand are a metaphor, may destroy the belief.

3. *Constitutionalism Made Concrete*

EARLY in the history of Western society, political thinkers in Rome hit upon the idea that the concepts of the public philosophy—particularly the idea of reciprocal rights and duties under law—could be given concreteness by treating them as contracts. In this way, freedom emanating from a constitutional order has been advocated, explained, made real to the imagination and the conscience of Western men; by establishing the presumption that civilized society is founded on a public social contract.

A contract is an agreement reached voluntarily, *quid pro quo,* and likely, therefore, to be observed—in any event, rightfully enforceable. Being voluntary, it has the consent of the parties. The presumption is not only that one party has acceded to what the other party proposed, but also that, in the original meaning of the word, both parties have consented—that they have thought, felt and judged the matter together.[6] Being a contract, the agreement will, presumably, be specific enough to minimize the quarrels of misunderstanding. It will say what the parties may expect of one another. It will say what are their respective rights and duties. In the field of the contract, their relations will be regulated and criteria will exist for adjudicating issues between them.

These are the essential characteristics of a constitutional system. It can be said to prevail when every man in and out of office is bound by lawful contracts. Without this, that is without constitutional government, there is no freedom. For the antithesis to being free is to be at the mercy of men who can act arbitrarily. It is not to know what may be done to you. It is to have no right to an accounting, and to have no means of objecting. Despotism and anarchy prevail when a constitutional order does not exist. Both are lawless and arbitrary. Indeed, despotism may be defined as the anarchy of lawless rulers, and anarchy as the despotism of lawless crowds.

The first principle of a civilized state is that power is legitimate only when it is under contract. Then it is, as we say, duly constituted. This principle is of such controlling significance that in the Western world the making of the contracts of government and of society has usually been regarded as marking—historically or symbolically—the crossing of the line which divides barbarity from civility.

Yet, as a matter of fact, there were not many actual documents. The public men who developed the constitutional systems of the West had a few texts, actually signed and sealed and delivered, to work with. There were, says Gierke, some "actual contracts between German princes and the estates of their realms." There are the celebrated contracts like Magna Carta, the Bill of Rights, the American Constitution. But genuine historic contracts are scarce, and they do not begin to cover all the political powers that need to be regulated.

There are not and never have been, and indeed could never be, specific contracts covering the unwritten laws of the good society, covering the domain of manners, as Lord Moulton called it, which includes "all things that a man should impose upon himself, from duty to good

---

[6] Cf. *Encyclopedia of Religion and Ethics,* Vol. IV, article "Consent."

taste."[7] It is necessary somehow to give authority to these unwritten laws, to invest them in some way with the reality of concreteness. The public philosophers drew by analogy upon the Roman Law, which presumed that in certain cases an agreement had been reached and an obligation incurred by acts unaccompanied by any express pact (*quasi ex contractu*).[8]

The general idea that the unwritten laws of public behavior are contractual and rest on consent was materialized in myths of an original covenant entered into by the first ancestors and binding upon their descendants. These myths, which appear in many versions at various times and places, make credible—by materializing it— the ethereal notion that civility is a fabric of understandings. The Ark of the Covenant, says Deuteronomy, contained the two tables of stone on which were written with the finger of God the Ten Commandments. Now, as a matter of fact, the Ark and the two tables of stone did not exist when Deuteronomy was compiled. But if they had never existed, how would the authors of Deuteronomy have convinced the Israelites that they must obey the Ten Commandments? They would not have gotten much obedience to the Commandments if they had told the Israelites that it was not certain, but merely probable, that they had been drawn up by Moses himself, and that it could be assumed that the Commandments reflected the considered judgment of Moses of how best to promote the greatest happiness of the greatest number of Israelites. The Ten Commandments had a better chance of being obeyed by the Israelites if they were written by God, rather than by another Israelite. And it was easier to believe that God did write them if, once upon a time, the two tables of stone had been deposited in the Ark of the Covenant.

Many in the modern age have rejected the idea of the contractual basis of power because, as a matter of fact, there never was an historic contract. Bentham, for example, knew that the two tables of stone could not be found and he wrote that "the origination of governments from a contract is a pure fiction, or in other words a

[7] Lord Moulton, "Law and Manners," in *Atlantic Monthly* (July 1924).

[8] Charles Howard McIlwain, *The Growth of Political Thought in the West* (1932), p. 118.

falsehood . . . where it is but from government that contracts derive their binding force?"[9]

To this we must reply that a fiction is not necessarily a falsehood. It may be the vehicle of a truth. Where do governments derive the power, which Bentham speaks of, to bind contracts? Only where the governments are conducted by men in a community who feel themselves bound by the belief that contracts are binding. The laws prevail when the lawmakers and the judges and the law enforcers are attached to the laws. When they are not attached to the laws, the laws of contract and the laws of the rights of man—the laws of the constitution, of charters, of treaties—are a dead letter, like, for example, the encyclopedic bill of rights in the Soviet Constitution of 1936.

"The personal liberty of the individual," says Blackstone, in the celebrated chapter on "The Legal Rights of Englishmen,"[10] is protected in part by the Habeas Corpus Act, which provides that "no subject of England can be long detained in prison" unless it can be proved in court that he is lawfully imprisoned. "Lest this act should be evaded by demanding unreasonable bail or sureties for the prisoner's appearance, it is declared . . . that excessive bail ought not to be required."

But the Habeas Corpus Act, which is a legal device to protect the personal liberty of the individual, does that— obviously enough—only where and when it is observed and enforceable. That will be only in a country where the executive and the assembly, the judges, the jailers and the lawyers feel bound, as if by personal contract, to the principles of the Habeas Corpus Act. Otherwise, no matter what the words of the law, it can happen to anyone, as to the man in Kafka's story, that he might never find out why he was in prison. Blackstone could not have written with such assurance that the Habeas Corpus Act prevents arbitrary detention in prison if in the England of his time the rights and duties that the Act declares had not become concrete and real, had not become matters of genuine concern.

---

[9] Jeremy Bentham, *Anarchical Fallacies; Being an Examination of the Declaration of Rights Issued During the French Revolution*, Art. II, Sentence 1.

[10] *Commentaries*, Book I, Chapter 1, 2.

4. *The Language of Accommodation*

MEN HAVE been laboring with the problem of how to make concrete and real what is abstract and immaterial ever since the Greek philosophers began to feel the need to accommodate the popular Homeric religion to the advance of science. The theologians, says Aristotle, are like the philosophers in that they promulgate certain doctrines; but they are unlike them in that they do so in mythical form.[11]

The method of accommodation employed by the philosophers has been to treat the materialization in the myth as allegory: as translation of the same knowledge into another language.[12] To converse with the devil, for example, could then mean what literally it says—to talk face to face with the devil, a concrete materialized personage. But it could mean, also, the imitation of a wicked nature without—as the Cambridge Platonist John Smith wrote, "a mutual local presence,"[13] that is to say without meeting a devil in person. This was an accommodation to those who, believing in the wickedness of evil, could not believe in the personified devil. The devil could mean either "some apostate spirit as one particular being," and also "the spirit of apostasie which is lodged in all men's natures." This is the method of plural interpretation; it uses "the language of accommodation." It is justified and legitimate, said John Smith in his discourse entitled "A Christian's Conflicts and Conquests," because "truth is content, when it comes into the world, to wear our mantles, to learn our language, to conform itself as it were to our dress and fashions . . . it speaks with the most idiotical sort of men in the most idiotical way, and becomes all things to all men, as every sonne of truth should do for their good."[14]

---

[11] Werner Jaeger, *The Theology of the Early Greek Philosophers* (The Gifford Lectures, 1936), p. 10. Cf. Aristotle, *Metaphysics*, Bk. III, Ch. 4, 1000a 4-18.

[12] Cf. Basil Willey, *The Seventeenth Century Background* (1952), Ch. IV.

[13] *Ibid.*, p. 138 *et seq.*

[14] *Ibid.*, p. 146.

5. The Limits of Accommodation

BUT THERE are limits beyond which we cannot carry the time-honored method of accommodating the diversity of beliefs. As we know from the variety and sharpness of schisms and sects in our time, we have gone beyond the limits of accommodation. We know, too, that as the divisions grow wider and more irreconcilable, there arise issues of loyalty with which the general principle of toleration is unable to cope.

For the toleration of differences is possible only on the assumption that there is no vital threat to the community. Toleration is not, therefore, a sufficient principle for dealing with the diversity of opinions and beliefs. It is itself dependent upon the positive principle of accommodation. The principle calls for the effort to find agreement beneath the differences.

In studying how accommodation is achieved, we may begin by observing that it is the philosophers, using Aristotle's broad terminology, who work out and promote the plural interpretation. They propose the terms for accommodating their immaterial belief to the concrete and materialized imagery of the fundamentalists. Thus it was the Cambridge Platonist, John Smith, who took the initiative about the devil. John Smith was not addressing the fundamentalists who believed in the personified devil; in fact what he said about the whole matter was not meant to trouble the fundamentalists at all. He was addressing men who were unable to believe in the personified devil and yet were still in essential communion with the fundamentalists. For they did believe in the spirit of the devil which, as everyone knows, is in all of us. In this accommodation the Christian Platonists gave up trying to believe what they could not believe. They went on believing that which in its essence their fundamentalist neighbors believed. Thus they could continue to live in the same community with them.

There is an impressive historical example of how by accommodation it is possible to communicate these difficult truths to a large heterogeneous society. In mediaeval Christendom a great subject of accommodation was the origin and sanction of the public philosophy itself, of the natural laws of the rational order. Otto von Gierke says that despite the innumerable learned controversies of the lawyers, the theologians and the philosophers, "all were agreed that there was natural law, which, on the one hand, radiated from a principle transcending earthly power, and on the other hand was true and perfectly binding law . . . the highest power on earth was subject to the rules of natural law. They stood above the Pope and above the Kaiser, above the ruler and above the sovereign people, nay, above the whole community of mortals. Neither statute nor act of government, neither resolution of the people nor custom, could break the bounds that thus were set. Whatever contradicted the eternal and immutable principles of natural law was utterly void and would bind no one."[15]

But though there was agreement on this, there was deep controversy over whether the natural laws were the commands of God or whether they were the dictates of an eternal reason, grounded on the being of God, and unalterable even by God himself. How were men to imagine, to materialize and make concrete the natural law which is above the Pope and the Kaiser and all mortals? As decrees of an omniscient and omnipotent heavenly king? Or as the principles of the nature of things? There were some who could not conceive of binding laws which had to be obeyed unless there was a lawgiver made in the image of the human lawgivers they had seen or heard about. There were others to whose capacity it was not necessary to condescend with quite that much materialization.

The crucial point, however, is not where the naturalists and supernaturalists disagreed. It is that they did agree that there was a valid law which, whether it was the commandment of God or the reason of things, was transcendent. They did agree that it was not something decided upon by certain men and then proclaimed by them. It was not someone's fancy, someone's prejudice, someone's wish or rationalization, a psychological experience and no more. It is there objectively, not subjectively. It can be discovered. It has to be obeyed.

[15] Otto von Gierke, *Political Theories of the Middle Age,* translated with an Introduction by Frederick William Maitland (Cambridge University Press, 1927). Cf. pp. 73-87 and more especially Note 256.

6. The Death of God

As LONG, then, as both the philosopher and the theologian believe in the objective order, there can be accommodation about the degree and kind of materialization. The range and variety of men's capacity to understand is very great. So, too, must be the range and variety of the images which condescend to their varying capacities. We can, therefore, avoid much misunderstanding if we do not confound the materialization—which is the mode of communicating belief—with the subject of the belief. For not until we go down under the comparatively superficial question of belief or unbelief, in any particular materialization, do we find the radical problems of belief and unbelief.

When Martin Buber speaks of "the great images of God fashioned by mankind."[16] he recognizes that there can be many images, or indeed that there can be no image which has concreteness to our sense perceptions.

The critical question does not turn on whether men do or do not believe in an imagery. It turns on whether they believe that a man is able "to experience a reality absolutely independent of himself." When Sartre, following Nietzsche, says that "God is dead," the critical point is not that he refuses to believe in the existence, however attenuated, of an anthropomorphic God. There can be, indeed there is, great faith and deep religion without any concrete image of God. The radical unbelief lies underneath the metaphor of God's death. It is in Sartre's saying that "if I have done away with God the Father, someone is needed to invent values . . . life has no meaning *a priori* . . . it is up to you to give it a meaning, and value is nothing but the meaning that you choose."[17]

With this, Sartre has done away not only with God the Father but with the recognition that beyond our private worlds there is a public world to which we belong. If what is good, what is right, what is true, is only what the individual "chooses" to "invent," then we are outside the

[16] Martin Buber, *Eclipe of God* (1952), p. 22.
[17] Jean Paul Sartre, *Existentialism*, translated by Bernard Frechtman (1947), p. 58. See also Martin Buber, *op. cit.*, p. 93.

traditions of civility. We are back in the war of all men against all men. There is left no ground for accommodation among the varieties of men; nor is there in this proclamation of anarchy a will to find an accommodation.

And why, we may ask, is there among such modern philosophers as these no concern like that of their great predecessors, to find an accommodaton? It is not only because they themselves have ceased to believe in the metaphors—in the sacred images. They have ceased to believe that behind the metaphors and the sacred images there is any kind of independent reality that can be known and must be recognized.

Thus they reject "the concept of 'truth' as something dependent upon facts largely outside human control," which, as Bertrand Russell says, "has been one of the ways in which philosophy hitherto has inculcated the necessary element of humility. When this check upon pride is removed, a further step is taken on the road towards a certain kind of madness—the intoxication of power which invaded philosophy with Fichte . . . and to which modern men, whether philosophers or not, are prone. I am persuaded that this intoxication is the greatest danger of our time, and that any philosophy which, however unintentionally, contributes to it is increasing the danger of vast social disaster."[18]

7. *The Mandate of Heaven*

AT THE end, then, the questions are how we conceive of ourselves and the public world beyond our private selves. Much depends upon the philosophers. For though they are not kings, they are, we may say, the teachers of the teachers. "In the history of Western governments," says Francis G. Wilson,[19] "the transitions of society can be marked by the changing character of the intellectuals," who have served the government as lawyers, advisers, administrators, who have been teachers in the schools, who have been members of professions like medicine and theology. It is through them that doctrines are made to

[18] Bertrand Russell, *History of Western Philosophy* (1945), p. 828.
[19] Francis G. Wilson, "Public Opinion and the Intellectuals," in *American Political Science Review* (June 1954).

operate in practical affairs. And their doctrine, which they, themselves, have learned in the schools and universities, will have the shape and the reference and the direction which the prevailing philosophy gives it.

That is how and why philosophy and theology are the ultimate and decisive studies in which we engage. In them are defined the main characteristics of the images of man which will be acted upon in the arts and sciences of the epoch. The role of philosophers is rarely, no doubt, creative. But it is critical, in that they have a deciding influence in determining what may be believed, how it can be believed, and what cannot be believed. The philosophers, one might say, stand at the crossroads. While they may not cause the traffic to move, they can stop it and start it, they can direct it one way or the other.

I do not contend, though I hope, that the decline of Western society will be arrested if the teachers in our schools and universities come back to the great tradition of the public philosophy. But I do contend that the decline, which is already far advanced, cannot be arrested if the prevailing philosophers oppose this restoration and revival, if they impugn rather than support the validity of an order which is superior to the values that Sartre tells each man "to invent."

What the prevailing philosophers say about religion is not itself, in Tillich's terms, religion as an ultimate concern of worship and of love. But if the philosophers teach that religious experience is a purely psychological phenomenon, related to nothing beyond each man's psychic condition, then they will give educated men a bad intellectual conscience if they have religious experiences. The philosopher cannot give them religion. But they can keep them away from it.

Philosophers play the same role in relation to the principles of the good society. These require, as we have seen, the mastery of human nature in the raw by an acquired rational second nature. In the literal sense, the principles of the good society must be unpopular until they have prevailed sufficiently to alter the popular impulses. For the popular impulses are opposed to public principles. These principles cannot be made to prevail if they are discredited,—if they are dismissed as superstition, as obscurantism, as meaningless metaphysics, as reactionary, as self-seeking rationalizations.

The public philosophy is in a large measure intellectually discredited among contemporary men. Because of that, what we may call the terms of discourse in public controversy are highly unfavorable to anyone who adheres to the public philosophy. The signs and seals of legitimacy, of rightness and of truth, have been taken over by men who reject, even when they are not the avowed adversaries of, the doctrine of constitutional democracy.

If the decline of the West under the misrule of the people is to be halted, it will be necessary to alter these terms of discourse. They are now set overwhelmingly against the credibility and against the rightness of the principles of the constitutional state; they are set in favor of the Jacobin conception of the emancipated and sovereign people.[20]

I have been arguing, hopefully and wishfully, that it may be possible to alter the terms of discourse if a convincing demonstration can be made that the principles of the good society are not, in Sartre's phrase, invented and chosen—that the conditions which must be met if there is to be a good society are there, outside our wishes, where they can be discovered by rational inquiry, and developed and adapted and refined by rational discussion.

If eventually this were demonstrated successfully, it would, I believe, rearm all those who are concerned with the anomy of our society, with its progressive barbarization, and with its descent into violence and tyranny. Amidst the quagmire of moral impressionism they would stand again on hard intellectual ground where there are significant objects that are given and are not merely projected, that are compelling and are not merely wished. Their hope would be re-established that there is a public world, sovereign above the infinite number of contradictory and competing private worlds. Without this certainty, their struggle must be unavailing.

As the defenders of civility, they cannot do without the signs and seals of legitimacy, of rightness and of truth. For it is a practical rule, well known to experienced men, that the relation is very close between our capacity to act at all and our conviction that the action we are taking is right. This does not mean, of course, that the action *is* necessarily right. What is necessary to continuous action is that it shall be *believed* to be right.

[20] Cf. Chapter Seven.

Without that belief, most men will not have the energy and will to persevere in the action. Thus satanism, which prefers evil as such, is present in some men and perhaps potential in many. Yet, except in a condition of the profoundest hysteria, as in a lynching, satanism cannot be preached to multitudes. Even Hitler, who was enormously satanic and delighted in monstrous evil, did nevertheless need, it would seem, to be reassured that he was not only a great man but, in a mysterious way, a righteous one.

William Jennings Bryan once said that to be clad in the armor of righteousness will make the humblest citizen of all the land stronger than all the hosts of error.[21] That is not quite true. But the reason the humblest citizen is not stronger than the hosts of error is that the latter also are clad in an armor which they at least believe is the armor of righteousness. Had they not been issued the armor of righteousness, they would not, as a matter of fact, be a host at all. For political ideas acquire operative force in human affairs when, as we have seen, they acquire legitimacy, when they have the title of being right which binds men's consciences. Then they possess, as the Confucian doctrine has it, "the mandate of heaven."

In the crisis within the Western society, there is at issue now the mandate of heaven.

[21] Speech at Democratic National Convention (Chicago, 1896).

Index

teenth century, 21-22

Foster, James R., cited, 125n.

Four Freedoms, 26

France, 50; decisions of the thirties, 23; enfranchisement of the people in, 37-38; failure to avert war, 11-12; governing class in, 55; manpower losses, 17n.; mutinies in, 17

Francis Joseph, Emperor, 17

Franco-Prussian War, 16

Free institutions, destroyed in counterrevolutionary movements, 101; inseparable from public philosophy, 101-103

Freedom, achievement of religious, 76; changed meaning of, 78-79; current theory of, 88; definitions, 110-111; deranged democratic governments a threat to, 32

Freedom of speech, limits of dissent, 101-103; modern abuses caused by lack of debate, 99-101; purpose and justification of, 96-99

French Revolution, 77; Jacobin doctrine in, 56

Froebel, F. W. A., on will of child, 75

Fromm, Erich, 85; on education, 74

GALLUP POLLS, and public policy, 39-40

George III, 57, 58

Germany, 50; July crisis, 17; National Socialist counterrevolution, 51; rebellion against peace settlement in, 26

Gide, André, 86; on feeling freedom, 85

Gierke, Otto von, 83n., 128; on belief in natural law, 76, 132, 133n.

Gilson, Étienne, cited, 105n.; on dissolution of Western culture, 85

Godwin, William, on reason, 64

Government, basis of constitutional, 127-128; relationship of executive and representatives in, 30-31; role of people in, 19-20; tendency to please the voters in, 42

Great Britain, 49; decisions of the thirties, 23; enfranchisement of the people in, 37-38, 55-56; failure to avert war, 11-12; in First World War, 17n., 17; in Second World War, 26; nineteenth century foreign policy, 21-22

Greece, traditions lost in, 81-82

HAAS, ERNST B., 119-120

Habeas Corpus Act, 130-131

Hamilton, Alexander, 28n., 45n., 47n.

Hapsburg Empire, collapse of, 14

Henry III, Parliament summoned by, 30

Hitler, Adolph, 23, 25, 68, 71, 138; on the masses, 86

Hobbes, Thomas, freedom defined, 110; on balance of power, 120

Hocking, William Ernest, on adaptability of humans, 75

Hohenzollern Empire, collapse of, 14

Holbach, Paul Heinrich von, on unjust rulers, 56

Holmes, Justice Oliver Wendell, 96

Hooker, Richard, on Puritan revolutionaries, 70

IDEAS, efficacy of, 72-75

Italy, 50; Fascist counterrevolution, 51

Ius civile, 83

Ius gentium, 83-84, 89

Ius naturale, 84, 89

JACKSON, ANDREW, 56

Jacobin revolution, doctrine of, 56

Jacobinism, and Leninism, 65-68; and liberalism, 54-70; as Christian heresy, 60-61; as popular theory in mass education, 61-65; as rebellion against governing caste, 58-59; public philosophy in contradiction to, 124-125

Jaeger, Werner, cited, 131n.

141

James, William, on change, 111, 112

Jaspers, Karl, 87, 105

Jay, John, cited, 45n., 47n.

Jefferson, Thomas, interest in government, 57-58; on role of people in democratic government, 19

Jesus, beginning of Christian law in precepts of, 114

Johnston, Sir Harry, on conduct of foreign affairs, 21-22

Justinian, 84

KORAN, 115

LAW, CHRISTIAN, 112-115; natural, 107-109, 132-133; Roman, 83-84

Lenin, Nikolay, 25, 71; as self-appointed agent of history, 68; revolutionary movement changed to totalitarianism by, 66-68

Leninism, from Jacobinism to, 65-68

Leo XIII, Pope, on orbit of church and state, 119

Liberalism, and Jacobinism, 54-70

Liberty. See Freedom

Lloyd George, David, 22

Locke, John, 77; on freedom, 111

MACDOUGAL, WILLIAM, on power of instinctive impulses, 64-65

Madison, James, 45n., 47n.

Magna Carta, 77, 128

Maine, Sir Henry, on duties of democratic government, 15; on fragility of popular government, 43

Marshall Plan, 23

Marx, Karl, 71, 94; debt to Jacobins, 59; on class struggle, 65

Mass opinion. See Public opinion

Mein Kampf, 86

Mill, John Stuart, 38n.; on free speech as means to truth, 98

Milton, John, on freedom of speech, 96-97

Montesquieu, Charles de, free-

dom defined, 111; on balance of power, 121

Moses, 129

Moulton, Lord, 128-129

Murray, John Courtney, S. J., on plurality of faiths, 76

Mussolini, Benito, 14, 23, 25

NATURAL LAW, belief in, 132-133; meaning of, 83-84; new school of, 84-85

Natural rights of man, progress of idea, 77

Nef, John U., on material progress of West, 16

Nevins, Allan, on early American elections, 33n.

Newman, Cardinal Henry, 106

Nicholson, Harold, 25

Nickerson, Hoffman, 17

Nietzsche, Friedrich Wilhelm, 134

OPINION. See Public opinion

Orlando, Vittorio Emanuele, 22

Ottoman Empire, collapse of, 14

PAGET, THIEBENNE, 125

Paine, Tom, 56

Paris Peace Conference, failure of, 25-26

Parliament, evolution of relationship between government and people in, 30-31

Peace, role of public opinion in, 25-27

Pearl Harbor, 26

People, alienated from public philosophy, 78-79, 80; as corporate being, 34-36; as understood in the Constitution, 32-34; communicating public philosophy to, 124-127; defined as voters or as community, 32-36; enfranchisement not implied in popular sovereignty, 36-37; inability to cope with freedom, 86-87; political power denied in counterrevolution, 51-52; represented in Parliament, 30-31; role in democracy, 19-20; tendency to choose authority, 52-53. See also Public opinion

142

St. Chrysostom, 115

St. John, 118

St. Mark, on miracle of Jesus, 126

St. Paul, on laws for the lawless, 110; on regeneration, 116

St. Thomas Aquinas. *See* Aquinas

Sartre, Jean Paul, 137; denial of God, 134

Schneider, Herbert W., 103*n.*

Schools, demands upon, 61-62. *See also* Education

Second World War, fatal cycle repeated in, 26; propaganda of, 26-27

Shaw, Bernard, on value of reasoning, 64

Simon, Yves R., on concentration of power in legislative body, 43*n.*

Slater, Rev. Thomas J., S. J., on development of Christian law, 114

Smith, John, 132; on truth, 131-132

Socrates, civilized nature of, 106-107

Soviet Constitution of 1936, 130

Spain, 50; Falangist counterrevolution, 51

Speech, freedom of, 96-101

Spengler, Oswald, 85-86

Spykman, Nicholas, on balance of power, 121

Stalin, Josef, 68, 71

Stoics. *See* Zeno

Strauss, Leo, 76*n.,* 88*n.*

Suffrage. *See* Universal suffrage

TAINE, HIPPOLYTE A., 56, 57, 59-60

Talmon, J. C., 54*n.,* 67*n.*

Talmud, 115

Ten Commandments, 129

Tillich, Paul, 178; on belief in God, 126

Titoist counterrevolution, 51

Tocqueville, Alexis de, impressions of democracy, 54-55

Totalitarianism, as understood by Lenin, 66-68. *See also* Counterrevolution

Toynbee, Arnold, 75, 88

UNITED KINGDOM. *See* Great Britain

United States, enfranchisement in, 38, 56; foreign policy before First World War, 21-22; indecision during Second World War, 11-12; 22-23; 26; Jacobinism in, 56. *See also* American Revolution of 1776

United States Senate, toleration of opinion in, 100

Universal suffrage, advanced toward, 37-38; effect on public opinion, 37; not implied in popular sovereignty, 36-37; preceded by Bill of Rights, 38

U.S.S.R. *See* Russia

VICTORIA, QUEEN, 21

Voegelin, Eric, 67*n.*

Voltaire, François Marie de, 60

Voters, opinions and the public interest, 39-40; versus the community, 32-35

WALLAS, GRAHAM, 16

War, role of public opinion in, 25-26. *See also* First World War, Second World War

Washington, George, 28*n.*

Westermarck, Edward A., 115*n.*

Western democracies. *See* Democracies

Western Europe, defeats in Second World War, 26

Western society, decline of, 13ff.

Willey, Basil, cited, 131*n.*

Wilson, Frank G., on influence of intellectuals in society, 135-136

Wilson, Woodrow, 13, 22, 45*n.*

World War. *See* First World War, Second World War

YALTA AGREEMENT, 25

ZENO, 81, 82, 89; common law formulated by, 82-83

Zernach, Ada, on de Tocqueville, 55*n.*